WARRIOR 3

AZTEC WARRIOR
AD 1325–1521

WRITTEN BY
JOHN POHL PhD
COLOR ILLUSTRATIONS BY
ADAM HOOK

OSPREY
MILITARY

First published in Great Britain in 2001 by Osprey Publishing, Elms Court, Chapel Way, Botley, Oxford OX2 9LP, United Kingdom.
Email: info@ospreypublishing.com

ISBN 1 84176 148 6

Editor: Nikolai Bogdanovic
Design: Ken Vail Graphic Design, Cambridge, UK
Index by Alan Rutter
Originated by Magnet Harlequin, Uxbridge, UK
Printed in China through World Print Ltd.

FOR A CATALOG OF ALL BOOKS PUBLISHED BY OSPREY MILITARY AND AVIATION PLEASE CONTACT:

The Marketing Manager, Osprey Direct USA,
c/o Motorbooks International, PO Box 1,
Osceola, WI 54020-0001, USA.
Email: info@ospreydirectusa.com

The Marketing Manager, Osprey Direct UK, PO Box 140,
Wellingborough, Northants, NN8 4ZA, United Kingdom.
Email: info@ospreydirect.co.uk

www.ospreypublishing.com

Artist's Note

Readers may care to note that the original paintings from which the color plates in this book were prepared are available for private sale. All reproduction copyright whatsoever is retained by the Publishers. All enquiries should be addressed to:

Scorpio Gallery, PO Box 475, Hailsham, East Sussex, BN27 2SL, UK.

The Publishers regret that they can enter into no correspondence upon this matter.

Editor's Note

The footnotes referred to in the text can be found on page 53.

TITLE PAGE **This priest has captured four of the enemy and has been awarded a variant of the Huaxtec uniform. The swirl of white dots on black signifies a celestial constellation over a night sky. (Author's illustration from *Codex Mendoza*)**

AZTEC WARRIOR
AD 1325–1521

INTRODUCTION

A child is sworn to service

STANDING BY THE FIRE at the middle of the narrow room, the infant's father looked on apprehensively as the mid-wife cut the umbilical cord and began to recite to his exhausted wife: "My beloved maiden, brave woman, you have returned from battle victorious." Then she held the baby up and pronounced: "Precious little jewel, here you are come into this world. War is your task. You shall give drink, nourishment and food to the sun and to the earth. There within the battlefield your name will be inscribed." When news of the birth spread throughout the neighborhood that night, the child's relatives quickly arrived bearing gifts and salutations. Then the tonalpouqui was summoned to read the augury. "The day of his birth is matlactli cuauhtli, ten eagle and it is a good sign for a soldier," declared the soothsayer after reading from the book of pictographics. "He will have strength and courage. He will spur others to valor. He will hurl himself against his foes, smash their ranks, and put terror into their hearts."(1) And so from the very night he was born, Cuauhtli was destined for a military career. His life and experiences would be shared by thousands of boys born under the day sign ten eagle throughout the 15th century when mandatory military service transformed what was once a small village of refugees called Tenochtitlan into the capital of the greatest military empire that the western hemisphere had ever known.

The story of Tenochtitlan

Cuauhtli would soon be taught the legacy of the Aztec people by his grandfathers. Aztlan, meaning Place of the Heron, was the legendary homeland of Chichimec tribes who miraculously emerged from seven caves located at the heart of a sacred mountain far to the north. They enjoyed a peaceful existence hunting and fishing until they were divinely inspired to fulfill a destiny of conquest. They journeyed until one day they witnessed a tree being ripped asunder by a bolt of lightning. The seventh and last tribe called the Mexica took the event as a sign that they were to divide and follow their own destiny. They continued to wander for many more years, sometimes hunting and sometimes settling down to farm, but never remaining in any one place for very long. After the collapse of the Toltec capital at Tula, they decided to move south to Lake Texcoco where they settled on the slopes of a mountain called Chapultepec. Impoverished and without allies, the Mexica were soon subjected to attacks by local Toltec warlords who forced them to retreat to an island where they witnessed a miraculous vision of prophecy; an eagle standing on a cactus. It was the sign for Tenochtitlan, their final destination. Having little to offer other than their reputation as fearsome

Much of what we know of the life of a soldier comes from the remarkable ethnographic studies of the Aztec civilization by Bernardino de Sahagún, a Franciscan friar who arrived in Mexico a few years after the fall of Tenochtitlan. He was fascinated by Indian customs and commissioned indigenous artists to paint images of what they remembered of their traditional life ways. The paintings were then used to illustrate his masterwork, *A General History of the Things of New Spain*, also known as the *Florentine Codex*. He wrote the manuscript in the Aztec language called Nahuatl. (Author's illustration from a Spanish colonial painting)

3

Using a folding book or codex, a tonalpouqui or soothsayer determines the prophecy of a child's future. Pictographs were composed of one of 20 day signs and up to 13 numerals. There is some indication that if the actual birth date had a poor prophecy, the tonalpouqui could designate a more favorable time. In effect this became a means by which priests assigned life's work to each member of a calpulli from birth. Ten Eagle was the 75th day of the 260-day count of a sacred divine calendar. Given that day was so propitious for warriors, there were undoubtedly many Ten Eagles in Aztec society. (Author's illustration from the *Florentine Codex*)

warriors, the Mexica had no other choice than to hire themselves out as mercenaries to rival Toltec factions. Eventually they were able to affect the balance of power in the region to such a degree that they were granted royal marriages. By the 15th century, this new Tolteca-Chichimeca aristocracy were calling themselves Aztecs after their divine place of origin.

Although Tenochtitlan was officially founded in 1325, it would be over a century before the city rose to its height as an imperial capital. Between 1372 and 1428 the Aztec huey tlatoque or "great speakers" Acamapichtli, Huitzilihuitl, and Chimalpopoca served as the vassals of a despotic lord named Tezozomoc of Azcapotzalco. Sharing in the spoils of victory they succeeded in expanding their own domain south and east along Lake Texcoco. However, when Tezozomoc died in 1427, his son Maxtla seized power and had Chimalpopoca assassinated. The Aztecs quickly appointed Chimalpopoca's uncle, a war captain named Itzcoatl, as tlatoani. Itzcoatl allied himself with the deposed heir to the throne of Texcoco, Lord Nezahualcoyotl. Together the two kings attacked Azcapotzalco. The siege lasted for over a hundred days and only concluded when Maxtla relinquished his throne and retreated into exile. Itzcoatl and Nezahualcoyotl then rewarded the Tepanec lords who had aided them in overthrowing the tyrant. The three cities of

Tenochtitlan, Texcoco, and Tlacopan formulated the new Aztec Empire of the Triple Alliance.

Itzcoatl died in 1440 and was succeeded by his nephew Motecuhzoma Ilhuicamina. Motecuhzoma I, as he was later known, charted the course for Aztec expansionism for the remainder of the 15th century. As a child, Cuauhtli would have listened intently to the stories of the campaigns of his forefathers and the vicious enemies that they had fought. To the west of the Basin of Mexico lay the formidable Tarascans who dominated a rich trade in luxury goods that moved along the Pacific coast by sea-going sailing rafts from South America to the Baja Peninsula. To the south and east were wealthy confederacies dominated by the Zapotecs, Mixtecs, and Eastern Nahuas, the latter being kinsmen of the Aztecs but no less bitter rivals for domination of the Southern Mexican highlands. The high priest Tlacaelel counseled Motecuhzoma that the imperial armies would fair better by first establishing bases of operation on the peripheries of these more powerful states. Motecuhzoma therefore initiated campaigns into Morelos and Guerrero from which his imperial armies could later launch sustained attacks for months or even years at a time.

Shortly after acceding to the throne, Motecuhzoma had demanded that all the city-states of the Basin of Mexico prove their loyalty to Tenochtitlan by contributing materials and labor for the construction of the Great Temple dedicated to the ancient Toltec storm god Tlaloc and the Chichimec hero Huitzilopochtli. Being allied with both the Mixtecs and the Eastern Nahua, the city-state of Chalco refused and this powerful

The Temple of the Warriors at Tollan (Tula, Hidalgo) the first Toltec capital. The atlantid figures are thought to represent either the Chichimec hero Camaxtli-Mixcoatl or his son Quetzalcoatl in the guise of the god of the Morning Star. (Author's photo)

kingdom was subjugated in 1453. Choosing to avoid a confrontation with the Eastern Nahuas of Tlaxcala directly, the Aztecs then moved against the Huaxtecs and Totonacs of the Atlantic Gulf Coast. Using a variety of ingenious strategies, imperial armies soon overran much of northern Veracruz thereby assuring the empire rich tribute in exotic shell, cotton, cacao, gold, and the priceless feathers of tropical birds. Alarmed by these bold encircling maneuvers, the Eastern Nahua prepared themselves for a direct attack against Tlaxcala, Huexotzinco, or even the great pilgrimage center of the Toltec man-god Quetzalcoatl at Cholula, but the Aztecs bided their time.(2)

In AD 1458, an Aztec imperial army initiated another "end run" marching 500 miles (800km) south from the Basin of Mexico to lay siege to the Mixtec kingdom of Coixtlahuaca, Oaxaca. According to various accounts the expedition was organized by Motecuhzoma Ilhuicamina to avenge the murder of 160 merchants by Coixtlahuaca's Lord Atonal. However, at 300,000, the invasion force was clearly intended as more than simply a punitive expedition. Atonal immediately summoned the help of numerous Mixtec kingdoms including Teposcolula, Tilantongo, and Tlaxiaco as well as the Eastern Nahua city-states of Cholula, Huexotzinco, and Tlaxcala with whom Coixtlahuaca was confederated; but the plea was sent too late. Coixtlahuaca was defeated before relief could arrive. Atonal was garroted and many of his men were captured and later sacrificed before the Great Temple of Tenochtitlan. Scores of city-states and kingdoms throughout Puebla and Oaxaca were stunned by the defeat. It was the beginning of the end of an era of unprecedented independence and prosperity throughout Mesoamerica.

Motecuhzoma was succeeded by his son Axayacatl in 1468. As a prince, the successor had proven himself a capable military commander by leading an expedition against the Zapotecs of Tehuantepec: now he sought to capitalize on the conquests of his illustrious father by entirely surrounding the kingdom of Tlaxcala and expanding imperial control over the Huaxtecs and Mixtecs. According to legend Axayacatl and his uncle Tlacaelel commissioned a new monument for Tenochtitlan's central religious precinct, a great round stone carved with the

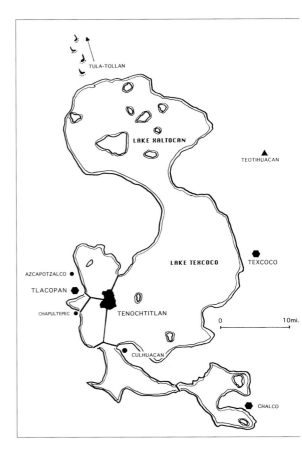

By AD 750, Teotihuacan, once a thriving metropolis of over 100,000 people, lay abandoned. According to legend early bands of Chichimecs then began to move into the region under the leadership of man-gods such Mixcoatl. Mixcoatl established the community of Culhuacan, then his son, Quetzalcoatl, founded a new capital at Tula 40 miles (64km) to the north-west. Eventually factional strife between rival Tula cults divided the Toltecs and many returned south to found new kingdoms along the shores of Lake Texcoco between AD 1000 and 1100. The last Chichimec tribe to arrive were the Mexica. After insulting the lord of Culhuacan, the Mexica were driven out on to an island in Lake Texcoco where they founded their own town of Tenochtitlan. The Basin of Mexico was subsequently dominated by the Tepanecs of Azcapotzalco throughout the early part of the 15th century and the Mexica thrived as their mercenaries. When the Tepanec tyrant Tezozomoc died, the throne was seized by Maxtla. Maxtla executed the Mexica king Chimalpopoca. The Mexica then elected Itzcoatl as king. Itzcoatl formulated an alliance with Nezahualcoyotl, the exiled heir to the Acolhua throne of Texcoco, and the two allies destroyed the Tepanec capital. Tepanecs loyal to the new order established a capital at Tlacopan and together the Mexicas, the Acolhuas, and the Tepanecs founded the Aztec Empire of the Triple Alliance. Itzcoatl's first campaigns were against Morelos in the south. Eventually the Aztecs turned on the Eastern Nahuas targeting the ancient city of Chalco. (Author's illustration)

image of the sun dedicated to war and the conquests of the empire. As tradition dictated they received aid in the form of materials and labor from Nezahualcoyotl of Texcoco, Totoquihuaztli of Tacuba, and the other Aztec city states:

> "Once this stone had been put in place, all the principal men who were present discussed the way the festivities would be held for the inauguration of the Sun Stone and where captives could be brought for sacrifice during these ceremonies. Axayacatl and Tlacaelel requested that their guests stay another day in Tenochtitlan so that they could propose to those allies that a war be waged against Michoacan." (Durán 1994: 277)

Michoacan, meaning Place of the Fishes, constituted the center of the Tarascan empire of over one million people ruled by an hereditary lord whose capital was located at Tzintzuntzan on Lake Patzcuaro. Although Axayacatl had mobilized an army of over 20,000 men he soon encountered a formidable Tarascan army nearly twice that size. Apprehensive but not deterred, Axayacatl directed his troops to attack. The battle raged throughout the day and well into the night. By the next morning, with the best of his shock troops dead or severely wounded, Axayacatl was forced to make a fighting retreat barely reaching Tenochtitlan with less than a fifth of his army still alive. The Sun Stone did not receive its promised tribute of hearts and blood and the defeat sent shock waves throughout the empire. Before long many city-states were rising in armed revolt in order to exploit the chaotic situation. By 1481, Axayacatl died. He was succeeded by Tizoc, who ruled briefly but ineffectually. Many suspect that he was even assassinated by members of his own court.

In 1486, the throne passed to Tizoc's younger brother, Ahuitzotl, who proved himself to be an outstanding military commander. Ahuitzotl reorganized the army and soon regained much of the territory lost under the previous administrations. He then initiated a program of long-distance campaigning on an unprecedented scale. By-passing the Tarascans he succeeded in conquering much of coastal Guerrero gaining free access to the strategic trade routes along the Pacific Coast through Acapulco. In 1497, he reconquered much of Oaxaca marching through Tehuantepec into Chiapas as far east as the Guatemalan border. Fearing that he would outdistance his sources of supply he then attempted to return but found that he had been betrayed by the Zapotecs. Only when he had agreed to an unprecedented royal marriage between the Zapotec king Cocijoeza and one his daughters, as well as ceding governorship over the newly conquered province of the Soconusco, was peace finally resolved. Nevertheless the empire reached its apogee under Ahuitzotl dominating as

The island on which the Mexica settled was originally divided between two communities, Tlatelolco and Tenochtitlan. During the reign of Axayacatl, however, Tlatelolco was subjugated following a dispute and its ceremonial precinct was incorporated as Tenochtitlan's principal market center. The city then became a natural fortress, virtually impregnable to outside attack. (Author's illustration)

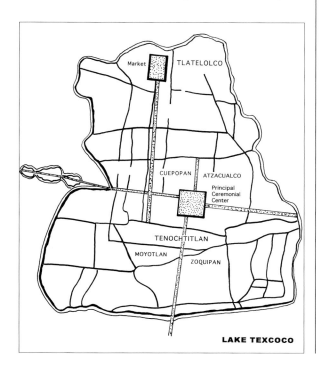

7

many as 25 million people throughout the Mexican highlands. When Motecuhzoma Xocoyotzin gained the throne in 1502, he too was eager to expand to the south and east attacking first the Mixtec coastal state of Tututepec and later sponsoring conquests to the east into Tabasco. By the time the first Spanish ships of the Córdova expedition of 1517 had been sighted off the Gulf Coast, Motecuhzoma II was ever contemplating an invasion of the kingdoms of the Maya on the Yucatan peninsula.

CHRONOLOGY OF PRINCIPAL EVENTS AD 1325–1521

1325 Tenochtitlan is founded by the Mexica, a tribe of Chichimec hunters, foragers, and expeditionary traders who had migrated into the Basin of Mexico from the northern deserts.

1371 Tezozomoc becomes the Tepanec tlatoani of Azcapotzalco and begins to subjugate rival Tolteca-Chichimeca city states surrounding Lake Texcoco with the help of the Mexica.

1372 Acamapichtli is made the first tlatoani of Tenochtitlan. The Culhuacan prince boasted a royal line extending directly back to the ancient Toltec capital of Tollan. He marries as many as 20 high-ranking Chichimec women whose children subsequently establish a class of hereditary Aztec nobility.

1375–1390 The Mexica conquer Xochimilco and Cuitlahuac, two ancient kingdoms. A ten-year series of Xochiyaoyotl "flower wars" are waged with Chalco.

1391–1417 Acamapichtli dies and is succeeded by Huitzilihuitl. Acting in league with Azcapotzalco, the Mexica conquer Xaltocan, Texcoco, Chalco, and other kingdoms to the east of Lake Texcoco.

1417–1425 Chimalpopoca, son of Huitzilihuitl and grandson of Tezozomoc accedes to the throne of Tenochtitlan. Texcoco's king Ixtlilxochitl is executed on the orders of Tezozomoc. His son, Nezahualcoyotl, flees to Tlaxcala.

1426 Tezozomoc dies. Chimalpopoca sides against Maxtla in his attempt to usurp the Tepanec throne of Azcapotzalco.

1427 Chimalpopoca is executed by Maxtla. Itzcoatl is appointed huey tlatoani.

1428 Itzcoatl allies himself with Nezahualcoyotl. Together they conquer Azcapotzalco and Tepanec overlords to found the Aztec Empire of the Triple Alliance.

1429–1439 Itzcoatl initiates campaigns against city-states in Morelos and Guerrero to reassert control over former Tepanec tributaries throughout the region.

1440 Itzcoatl dies and is succeeded by Motecuhzoma Ilhuicamina.

1441–1449 Motecuhzoma campaigns in Guerrero and engages in a protracted war against Chalco. The Basin of Mexico suffers a series of natural disasters including a devastating flood and a locust plague causing rampant food shortages.

1450–1454 A four-year famine devastates Tenochtitlan causing widespread death by starvation and the abandonment of the city by much of the population.

1455–1457 When prosperity returns, Motecuhzoma and his half-brother Tlacaelel mastermind a series of long-distance campaigns initiating attacks first against the Huaxtecs and Totonacs of what is today northern Veracruz. Flower wars are carried on with Tlaxcala.

1458	160 merchants are assassinated at Coixtlahuaca. An army of 300,000 is dispatched to punish the Mixtec kingdom in what would become the Aztec's first major long-distance campaign into southern Mesoamerica.
1468	Motecuhzoma dies and is succeeded by Axayacatl.
1472	Nezahualcoyotl, Texcoco's brilliant "scholar" king, dies and is succeeded by his son Nezahualpilli.
1473	Alarmed by the growing power of Tlatelolco, Axayacatl kills its tlatoani, Moquihuix, in personal combat and incorporates the former "sister" city into Tenochtitlan.
1480	The Aztec army suffers a devastating defeat at the hands of the Tarascans. The border is fortified and no subsequent emperor will ever attempt a direct attack against this formidable foe again.
1481–1486	Axayacatl dies and is succeeded by Tizoc. Tizoc is later assassinated. Many conquest states declare their independence from the empire.
1486–1488	Ahuitzotl accedes to the throne. He initiates a new series of campaigns against the Eastern Nahuas finally subjugating both Huexotzinco and Cholula. Tlaxcala is now entirely cut off from all of its former alliance partners.
1489–1491	Ahuitzotl embarks on a series of campaigns into coastal Guerrero in an attempt both to encircle the Tarascans and gain access to the lucrative Pacific coastal trade between Central America and the Baja Peninsula.
1491–1492	The Aztec army campaigns in southern Veracruz. Christopher Columbus lands at Hispañola (Haiti–Santo Domingo).
1494	Ahuitzotl leads a long distance campaign against the Mixtecs reconquering many rebellious kingdoms throughout the highlands.

1496–1497	Capitalizing on his successes in the Mixteca Alta, Ahuitzotl moves against the Zapotecs who eventually allow his army to pass through the Valley of Oaxaca to the Pacific Coast at Tehuantepec.
1499–1500	Ahuitzotl invades coastal Chiapas but decides not to press an attack against the Quiché and Cakchiquel Maya of highland Guatemala, choosing to return to Tenochtitlan instead.
1502	Ahuitzotl dies and is succeeded by Motecuhzoma Xocoyotzin.
1503–1515	The change in administration inspires rebellion among the Mixtecs. Successive campaigns of reconquest are directed against Achiutla, Jaltepec, Tlaxiaco, Yanhuitlan, Sosola, Tututepec, and Quetzaltepec among other kingdoms.
1515	Nezahualpilli, son of Nezahualcoyotl and tlatoani of Texcoco, dies. Motecuhzoma instigates a war of annihilation against Tlaxcala but is driven back in defeat.
1517	Hernandez de Córdoba leads the first Spanish expedition from Cuba to the Mexican Gulf Coast.
1518	Juan de Grijalva leads the second Spanish expedition to the Gulf Coast.
1519	Hernán Cortés invades Veracruz and marches on Tenochtitlan using Tlaxcala as a base of operations.
1520	Motecuhzoma is killed. Cortés is driven from Tenochtitlan and retreats to Tlaxcala. Cuitlahuac is appointed huey tlatoani but dies from smallpox. Cuauhtemoc then inherits the throne. Numerous disputes divide the city-states of the Basin of Mexico.
1521	In April, Cortés marches on Tenochtitlan at the head of an allied Indian army of over 50,000 troops. The battle for the city wages continuously over the course of five months. Tenochtitlan falls in August and Cuauhtemoc surrenders bringing an end to the Aztec Empire of the Triple Alliance.

EARLY YEARS – THE GENESIS OF THE WARRIOR

Despite the prophecy of his birth, Cuauhtli would have little to look forward to but a youthful life of toil. His education between the ages of three and fifteen was entrusted to his parents who taught him all that he should know of his calpulli (or town district) and the role that he should play in serving it. At first, Cuauhtli would spend years performing simple domestic tasks strengthening his body through heavy labor carrying wood, water, or supplies and food purchased in the market place at the center of the city. At seven he was trained to manage his family's boats and to fish on Lake Texcoco. When he wasn't participating in some ritual feast, Cuauhtli was encouraged to subsist on relatively meager amounts of food being given only a half a cake of maize per meal at age three, a full cake at age five, and a cake and a half at age twelve. One day he might have to march for days without any food at all. Punishments for idleness were severe and ranged from beatings to stinging with agave thorns or even having his face and eyes burned with the smoke of roasted chili peppers.

At 15, Cuauhtli considered applying to the calmecac or temple school where he would be trained for a life in the priesthood, but being born into a commoner family he decided to enter the telpochcalli, the young men's house run by masters chosen from amongst the calpulli's veteran warriors and a quicker route to advancement in the military. The day he arrived at the school his parents took him before the telpochtlato or "ruler" of the school and the sacred image of the god of the youths:

An early Aztec king awards a valiant warrior a xicalcoliuhqui shield, a tlahuiztli, a feather back ornament, and a cape ornamented with the pictograph for a star. (Author's illustration from *Codex Xolotl*)

"Here our lord has placed him. Here you understand, you are notified that our lord has given a jewel, a precious feather, a child has arrived. In your laps, in the cradle of your arms we place him. And now we dedicate him to the lord, shadow, wind, Tezcatlipoca and pray that he will sustain him. We leave him to become a young warrior. He will live here in the house of penance where the eagle warrior and the jaguar warrior are born."

(adapted from Sahagún 1950–1982 Book 3: 51–53)

In addition to his daily chores both at home and at the school, Cuauhtli was expected to cooperate with teams of other boys in public works particularly the cleaning and repairing of the aqueducts, canals, and causeways that criss-crossed the city and provided vital links for transportation. According to legend, the Mexica had once insulted the Toltec lord of Culhuacan who then drove the tribe out on to the small island off the western shore of Lake Texcoco. Here the forefathers had managed to survive by learning to fish and harvest a seasonal bounty of wild birds and other foodstuffs. Later the men of each calpulli organized themselves into teams and began to construct artificial fields called chinampas by cutting drainage canals through the marshes. Separate plots were staked off with poles lashed together with vines and filled with alternating layers of decomposing plants and fertile mud from the lake bed. Willow trees were then planted so that their roots could anchor each new plot to the lake bottom thereby inhibiting erosion. The

Three contemporary reconstructions of Aztec dress by the author. From left to right, a noble warlord wearing a yellow feather ehuatl and jaguar helmet, an otomi rank soldier wearing a green feather tlahuiztli, and the huey tlatoani Motecuhzoma II wearing the distinctive blue royal cloak or xiuhtlalpilli dyed or painted with glyphs signifying turquoise mosaic.

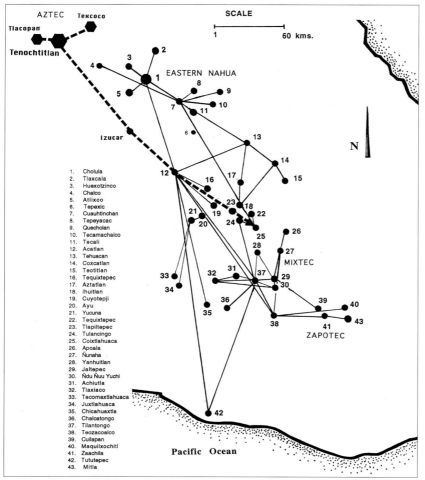

AZTEC Texcoco
Tlacopan
Tenochtitlan
Izucar

SCALE
1   60 kms.

2
3
4
1   EASTERN NAHUA
8
5   9
7   10
11
6   13
14
12   16   17   15
23
21   19   18   22
20   24
25   26
28   27
MIXTEC
31
33   32   37   29
34   30
39   40
36   43
35   38   41
ZAPOTEC

42
Pacific Ocean

N

1. Cholula
2. Tlaxcala
3. Huexotzinco
4. Chalco
5. Atlixco
6. Tepexic
7. Cuauhtinchan
8. Tepeyacac
9. Quecholan
10. Tecamachalco
11. Tecali
12. Acatlan
13. Tehuacan
14. Coxcatlan
15. Teotitlan
16. Tequixtepec
17. Aztatlan
18. Ihuitlan
19. Cuyotepji
20. Ayu
21. Yucuna
22. Tequixtepec
23. Tlapiltepec
24. Tulancingo
25. Coixtlahuaca
26. Apoala
27. Ñunaha
28. Yanhuitlan
29. Jaltepec
30. Ñdu Ñuu Yuchi
31. Achiutla
32. Tlaxiaco
33. Tecomaxtlahuaca
34. Juxtlahuaca
35. Chicahuaxtla
36. Chalcatongo
37. Tilantongo
38. Teozacoalco
39. Cuilapan
40. Maquilxochitl
41. Zaachila
42. Tututepec
43. Mitla

Between AD 1150 and 1450, the Eastern Nahuas, Mixtecs, and Zapotecs used royal marriages to create a confederacy that united their petty kingdoms throughout southern and eastern Mexico. Calling themselves the "Children of Quetzalcoatl" they maintained a great pilgrimage and merchant center at the city of Cholula (1). In planning their first long-distance campaign, the Aztec strategy was to break the back of the confederacy by first attacking Coixtlahuaca, the remotest link in the system, and then swallowing up the other kingdoms piecemeal. The dotted line illustrates the most likely route of attack. (Author's illustration)

chinampas were then fertilized by recycling the human waste from the community itself. This ingenious system of re clamation soon allowed the Mexica to grow as many as three crops of corn per years and to quadruple the island's land mass. The lake surrounding the island had supplied a natural barrier to enemy attack, a strategic advantage when the Mexica began to hire themselves out as mercenaries during the dry season. As wealth and prosperity increased, however, so did the need for a more permanent line of essential supply from trade with the kingdoms surrounding Lake Texcoco. An agreement was first arranged with Chapultepec to construct an aqueduct that brought fresh water to the city from where it had once had to be transported by canoe. Soon additional causeways were constructed that linked Tenochtitlan to both the northern and southern shores, but the Mexica had the forethought to incorporate a system of bridges that could be removed during periods of threat from outside attack. In this way the city could be transformed into a nearly impregnable fortress.

By the middle of the 15th century, the Mexica were growing rich in war tribute and the emerging elite sought to increase their rank and prestige by redistributing this new found wealth through a system of annual feasts dedicated to the pantheon of gods. In order to magnify the importance of these festivities they began to direct the construction of enormous temple and plaza precincts. The complexes served something like theaters for the reenactment of religious dramas that bound the families of each calpulli together both ritually and socially and it was here that both the priestly calmecac for the high born and the warrior telpochcalli for the commoner were located.

Many of the telpochcalli masters were hardly older than Cuauhtli himself. It was their job to watch and observe the new boys, looking out for those who were not only physically fit but showed respect and good judgment as well. Doubtless they intimidated the youths with insults and physical bullying as drill instructors have done in every army since time immemorial, but it was essential to determine who would thrive in the life

Eastern Nahua kingdoms consisted of dense populations of people living in large communities on the broad plain of Puebla. Their city-states were usually governed by a council of four tlatoque. This reconstruction illustrates a typical Nahua city center lying southeast of the Basin of Mexico with the volcanoes of Popocateptl and Iztac Cihuatl appearing on the horizon. (Author's illustration)

nd death situations of real combat. If Cuauhtli persevered he would be romoted to become a master of youths and perhaps later in life even a elpochtlato, a man responsible for training an entire generation of easoned warriors, upon which the empire depended for its survival. runkenness in general was forbidden in Aztec society and even unished with death. The most enjoyment a telpochcalli student might ope for throughout his Spartan life was the right to keep a mistress if he ould afford one.

Living at the telpochcalli, Cuauhtli had little time for the academic udies and religious exercises that were so important to the training of ne novitiate priests, children of prominent families that had been sent the calmecac. Everything was done strictly to prepare Cuauhtli for war nd back-breaking labor was the means by which he would be tested nroughout each and every day. The only relaxation he could enjoy was uring the evenings spent singing and dancing, exercises that would ond the boys of Cuauhtli's calpulli together spiritually as well as aining them in agility and coordination that would become so essential both hand-to-hand combat and troop movement. Many of the songs ere dedicated to the exploits of the gods, culture heroes, or warriors of ne calpulli who had accomplished great feats of heroism. Tezcatlipoca, ne school's patron, was believed to embody the most admirable values f a soldier. The god was bold and daring. He had used cunning to utwit his rival at Tollan, Quetzalcoatl, shaming him before his people nd banishing him from his realm. But there was a dark side to ezcatlipoca, even a sense of fatalism, for he was known to deceive his ollowers, instilling in them false pride only to withdraw his divine rotection when they needed it most and watch as they destroyed nemselves. It was surely no coincidence then that Quetzalcoatl was enerated as the patron god of the calmecac where the virtuous ideals of ne elite were emphasized through scholastic and devotional learning.

TRAINING

Boys were introduced to the actual violence of war through the principal religious festivals that were held throughout the year in Tenochtitlan's central ceremonial precinct. Towards the end of the dry season between February and April, festivals dedicated to both the storm god, Tlaloc, and the war god, Xipe Totec, were celebrated in Tenochtitlan's main ceremonial center before the Great Temple. Here thousands of people would gather to celebrate the conclusion of the "war time" and the onset of the planting season with feasting, dancing, and singing. The featured events however were the staged battles during which high ranking enemies captured during the previous campaign season fought for their lives in bloody gladiatorial combats against heavily armed opponents. At other times the students of both the calmecac and the telpochcalli were encouraged to participate in mock combats competing as teams against one another for food, gifts, and other rewards. Veteran warriors of different ranks and specialization taught the youths to handle all of the basic weapons such as slings, bows, arrows and spears. The more promising students were soon advanced to training in the use of the sword and shield.

No less essential to developing agility, speed, and endurance was the ball game, a sport dating to at least the second millennium BC. Once they had discovered the resilient properties of rubber, Mesoamericans created a variety of different versions of the game with competitions involving anywhere between one and ten men on a side. The game is still played in parts of Mexico today. The object is intensely territorial with two teams volleying the ball back and forth until one side is no longer able to keep it in the air. At the point where the ball hits the ground, referees mark the territory that is lost to the opposition. The match is forfeit when one team is driven so far into the end zone that they can no longer effectively maneuver. By late Aztec times the games bordered on social mania with elite and peasants alike wagering their entire fortunes

The rugged mountain terrain of Oaxaca was not conducive to dense settlement. Mixtec and Zapotec populations dispersed themselves over landscapes dominated by isolated royal palaces constructed on low-lying hills. During times of serious attack, the population often fled to the protection of more ancient fortifications built atop nearby mountains. (Author's illustration)

on the outcome of a single game. In some cases matches were actually played as an adjunct to war. Axayacatl provoked the king of Xochimilco into playing a ball game and wagered the tribute of a number of kingdoms around Lake Texcoco. When his opponent won the match, Axayacatl attacked and executed him.

Once Cuauhtli had proven himself both physically and mentally to his school masters he was recommended for recruitment. Being born during the reign of Ahuitzotl there would have been no shortage of opportunities to prove himself on the battlefield. His first assignment was to serve as a porter to an older boy from the calmecac who had recently succeeded in capturing a Huaxtec. Achievement in the Aztec Imperial army was dependent upon the number of captives that one took in battle and the status that each captive held among his own people. The Huaxtecs were frowned upon as relatively unworthy opponents and so those who captured them were not granted particularly rich rewards. A warrior who succeeded in capturing a Tlaxcalan on the other hand was highly revered. Consequently, Cuauhtli's mother was worried that this soldier wasn't experienced enough to protect her son. Everyone in the calpulli knew that the older boy had failed to take any captives at all after participating in three earlier battles. The school masters had even forced him to wear the cuexpalchicacpol or "baby's hairlock" in shame.

Students arrive at the telpochcalli or young men's house. Note the father speaking to a cuahchic about his boy. (Author's illustration from the *Florentine Codex*)

But there was little that Cuauhtli's family could do, as they did not have the money to offer a more experienced warrior like their wealthier neighbors, and so their son would have to watch out for himself.

In 1499, Cuauhtli proved himself for the first time in a Xochiyaoyotl or "Flower War" against Atlixco, a kingdom long contended by both the Aztecs and the Eastern Nahuas. Cuauhtli packed food, clothing, and supplies into a three-foot-high (0.91m) carrying basket for both himself and the older soldier. Then he bid his parents goodbye, picked up his shield and spear and marched across the Coyoacan causeway keeping a respectful distance behind the older soldier. The trip south into Puebla was not particularly arduous and the young men were well fed from stores strategically located

High ranking captives were often given the opportunity to defend themselves with mock weapons in gladiatorial combats before the Great Temple during the feast of Tlacaxipehualiztli. (Author's illustration from the *Florentine Codex*)

in communities all along the route of advance. By the time they reached Atlixco three days later, the Tlaxcalteca were already organized in densely packed squares ready to launch a frontal attack against the long thin battalion of Aztec skirmishers that had just begun to form up. Some of the cuahchic, or Shorn Ones, had already begun to engage the enemy attempting to draw out the foolhardy and thereby break open the dense enemy formation.

The exact function of the Xochiyaoyotl or Flower Wars are still debated by scholars. The Aztecs themselves maintained that they were fought both to train their soldiers and to acquire the much needed human offerings that their fearsome gods demanded. Originally the battles were waged something along the lines of the European Medieval mêlée. Emphasis was more on the display of prowess than the total defeat of the enemy. Novices foolish or careless enough to get captured got what they deserved. Furthermore, early Aztec politics was factional and any chance of escalating a Flower War into full combat was to be avoided: this year's foe might very well become next year's ally. The location of the contests was ordinarily predetermined through regular diplomatic channels and generals from both sides served as referees. By the late 15th century, however, Ahuitzotl was becoming increasingly desperate to defeat the Tlaxcalteca and their allies so battles between the rival armies at that time were beginning to be waged as "Flower Wars" in name only. Cuauhtli would have been astonished to see the Aztec army in full array at Atlixco each soldier going to great lengths to display his lavishly ornamented battle-gear, facial jewelry, and other gifts personally granted by a grateful emperor. He quickly helped the soldier he was assigned to escort into his armor, secured the shield to his arm and slipped the knot of his macuahuitl over his hand. Having performed his tasks dutifully, a senior captain then directed Cuauhtli to participate in the battle himself by wielding a long tepoztopilli from the rear of the line.

WEAPONRY AND PROTECTION

The weaponry with which Cuauhtli was trained had much in common with ancient armies throughout the world. The sons of farmers, the majority of the peasant population, would have been self-trained with the sling in order to supply the small game that thrived in the fields for the household dinner table. The weapon could be simply finger woven of maguey fiber, anywhere and at any time. A five-foot (1.52m) loop of cord was passed through a thong to hold the projectile in place. One end was wrapped around the three index fingers and the other was held between the forefinger and the thumb. Momentum was built up by swinging the loop over one's head four or more times and releasing the thumb at the point in the arc when the thong was oriented toward a target. Employed in actual combat, the sling was capable of propelling small oval stones specifically selected for their aerodynamics straight through a man's skull in excess of a range of 200 yards.

Being the original weapons of their Chichimec ancestors, boys were trained in the use of the bow and arrow and they practiced their skill in group hunts held in the surrounding mountains during the religious festival of Quecholli. Bows varied in length depending on their intended use, the longest being up to five feet (1.52m). The best were made of hickory and ash wood, the strings were made from raw hide or animal tendons. Arrows were generally made from viburnum and straightened by repeated applications of moisture and heat. The "nock" or end of the shaft had two or three feathers attached to it to direct the arrow's flight. A cleft was made in the front end of the shaft and the point was glued with pitch adhesive and lashed into place. Points were made of a variety of chert or flint, but copper and obsidian were used as well. Three-pronged bone arrow points ordinarily used for bird hunting would have inflicted particularly vicious wounds. Bowmen and slingers were essentially equal in their capacity to wreak havoc on the enemy from a distance and were frequently paired in units. However they were seldom employed as pivotal units for they were prone to be overrun and slaughtered at close range by more heavily armed opponents. They ordinarily took their places forward in order to shower the enemy with a barrage at the opening of an attack and then withdrew to the rear or flanks to lay down harassing fire as the troops began to engage in hand-to-hand combat.

The two shrines situated at the top of the Great Temple of Tenochtitlan were dedicated to the old Toltec storm god Tlaloc (left) and the Chichimec hero Huitzilopochtli (right). (Author's illustration from _Codex Borbonicus_)

Unquestionably, Mesoamerica's most ancient weapon was the spear together with the spear thrower or atlatl. It now appears that the Clovis atlatl spear-point tradition of Paleo-Indian times was actually introduced by Solutrian peoples engaged in coastal umiak hunting for walrus and whale between northern Spain and North America around 16,000 BC. The subsequent advantage of using spear throwers on land was that they allowed coordinated groups of hunters to launch repeated debilitating attacks against large creatures like bison and mammoth without having to engage them physically. Aztec spear throwers ranged in size but most surviving examples are about two feet (0.61m) in length. The thrower was grasped by slipping the first and second fingers through two loops either carved or lashed to the sides. The butt end of the spear was cradled into a depression that ran the length of one side. By casting the thrower forward with a whip-like motion the spear was launched against a target with as much as 20 times the force of arm strength alone. Many were magnificently carved from hard wood in a wide variety of ornamental designs. Serpents were especially favored and endowed the instrument with the spiritual qualities of a living being; and so they are sometimes described in legends. Despite its widespread use by the Teotihuacanos, Mixtecs, Zapotecs, and Maya, there is some debate as to how much the average Aztec soldier relied on the atlatl. It appears to have taken considerable practice to master and was therefore considered more of an elite weapon. It is notable therefore that it appears most frequently in the hands of Aztec gods.

Clubs and axes were widely employed. Roundhead clubs called cuauhololli were carved of hard wood. They were fairly easy to produce and were especially favored by the Huaxtecs, Tarascans and other foreign peoples. Their intent was to knock a man unconscious until he could be hog-tied up and moved to the rear of the line. Axes were probably as old as the spear thrower. Utilitarian in their origin, they appear in early Olmec art dating to 1000 BC as war implements in the hands of paramount chiefs. Axes were produced either of ground stone or cast copper and wedged into the perforated aperture of a wooden handle. These heavy weapons appear to have been used in earlier times as a preferred elite weapon for closing in on an opponent following a spear fight with the atlatl. Their employment by later Aztec imperial troops, however, was probably not widespread.

By far the single most important weapon used by Aztec soldiers was the macuahuitl, a kind of saw-sword carved of wood and affixed with an edge of obsidian razor blades and bitumen adhesive. Most examples were about three and a half feet (1.06m) long but others were of such size that they had to be wielded with both hands. It appears infrequently if at all in Mesoamerica during earlier times when war was more of an elite activity, so we presume that its widespread use among the Aztecs emerged in response to the need to arm and train large armies of commoners as quickly and efficiently as possible. During the Conquest, one Spaniard described seeing "an Indian fighting against a mounted man, and the Indian gave the horse of his antagonist, such a blow in the breast that he opened it to the entrails, and it fell dead on the spot. And the same day I saw another Indian give another horse a blow to the neck that stretched it out dead at his feet." From such accounts we learn that the macuahuitl had little other purpose than to severely maim if not actually dismember the enemy. The Aztecs also employed a closely related weapon called a tepoztopilli as a halberd. These were carved from wood and featured a long, wide, wedge-shaped head fitted with a row of obsidian blades much like the macuahuitl. They varied in length from three to seven feet (1.06–2.13m) in length. Cuauhtli would have been assigned to wield such a weapon during his first battlefield experiences. It allowed him to stand at the rear of the line and shove or jab the weapon, harassing the enemy from a safe distance while the more experienced warriors fought in hand-to-hand combat at the front of the line.

The Aztecs did not have so much of a Stone Age culture as an obsidian culture. Obsidian is a volcanic glass formed by the rapid cooling and solidification of the silica-rich parts of extruded lava. Often thick vents of obsidian are subject to erosion, so that concentrations of rolled and battered nodules appear in vast surface deposits, the largest of which were located around Tulancingo, 65 miles (105km) north-east of Tenochtitlan. Easily transported back to the city, the nodules were reduced to "cores" in the market places and distributed to hundreds of craft specialists who manufactured arrow points, knife blades, spear heads, and thousands of micro-blades used both for utilitarian and military purposes. Obsidian is a disposable technology, the antithesis of

Codex Mendoza was commissioned by New Spain's first viceroy for presentation to Charles V. It eventually fell into French hands, possibly through pirates, and now resides at the University of Oxford. It includes an excellent pictorial account of the lives of soldiers. Here a high ranker is shown marching with a shield ornamented with feathers and a pointed war stick called a huitzoctli. He is escorted by a youth of the telpochcalli carrying food and supplies for the two as well as his own weapons in a heavy woven basket. The third soldier is armed with a tepoztopilli, something like a halberd. He carries a cacaxtli, or carrying frame, to which are bound additional supplies together with cane for making arrow shafts. (Author's illustration from *Codex Mendoza*)

An axe head cast in solid copper. (Private collection)

expensive and labor intensive iron or steel. An obsidian worker can produce a blade in a matter of seconds, use it until it becomes dull or broken, and then simply strike a new blade to refit a weapon under virtually any kind of field conditions including combat itself.

The novel weaponry developed by the Aztecs fostered a need for equally ingenious forms of defense. For example, the vicious slashing and cutting that resulted from the macuahuitl necessitated the use of much larger shields than those used by earlier cultures. Circular shields called chimalli were generally about 30 inches (76cm) in diameter. The strongest were constructed of fire-hardened cane or wooden rods interwoven with heavy cotton. They were further decorated with a lower fringe of feather, leather, or cloth strips to provide additional protection to the legs. Others were composed of solid wood sometimes sheathed in copper. Shields were lavishly painted or ornamented with featherwork in a wide variety of heraldic designs that demonstrated the prowess of the owner, the most popular being the xicalcoliuhqui and cuexyo designs.

There were various forms of head protection and even the standard warrior's hairstyle or temilotl, formed by gathering up the hair of the top of the head to form a broad top-knot, would have impeded any direct blow to the skull considerably. Protective caps or hats were also worn with certain forms of battle dress. Elite warriors and field commanders commonly wore helmets of hard wood carved in the form of all sorts of fanciful creatures including jaguars, eagles, parrots, monkeys, wolves, and coyotes. They were constructed in such a way that they totally enveloped the head, something like an American football helmet, allowing the face to protrude through the opening in the heraldic patron's mouth to imply that the man was essentially one with his animal counterpart in religious belief. Nearly all soldiers wore armor jackets of cotton quilting called ichcahuipilli. As the Spaniards learned shortly after reaching Hispañola, metal armor was impractical in the hot, humid regions of the Caribbean, Mexico, and Central America. The ichcahuipilli was something more akin to a bullet-proof vest in that it was not designed to stop the force of a projectile on impact but rather absorb it. It came in many forms. The open-sewn garment could be worn like a jacket and tied in front with laces or ribbons. The closed-sewn garment was a vest that was pulled on over the head. Appearances of the ichcahuipilli in pictographic books indicate that they were worn in a variety of lengths from the waist to the calf. Most were left natural but some were dyed in bright colors. Cotton quilted jackets were frequently worn under or incorporated into an elite garment called the ehuatl, a

The author's reconstruction of a hefty five-foot (1.52m) long version of the macuahuitl. The weapon was secured to the wrist with a slip knot. The effectiveness of the sword was dependent upon razor sharp blades of obsidian struck from the platform of a prepared core.

closed sewn tunic made of cotton ornamented with animal skin or feathers. The ehuatl was also distinguished by a skirt of leather or cloth strips and feathers that protected the thighs. Aztec emperors were known to have favored an ehuatl of red spoonbill feathers when they personally took to the field. Arm and wrist bands as well as greaves of wood, bark, and leather sometimes sheathed in metal were generally worn with the ehuatl for additional protection.

DRESS AND DISTINCTION

When Cuauhtli joined the battle line at Atlixco, he must have been bewildered by the sheer variety of battledress. He would soon learn that these ritual garments actually composed the basis for a sophisticated system of uniform distinctions. In most cultures, uniforms are used to differentiate units, but in the Aztec army, uniforms served to differentiate men with different levels of military experience within the same unit. Nearly everyone in a xiquipilli or regiment was closely related because troops were recruited within the same calpulli neighborhood. Unit morale and mutual responsibilities were therefore dependent on family ties and it was the sworn duty of the veterans to look out for the recruits. The display of their lavish uniforms must have been a tremendous symbol of pride and encouragement to the youths who fought alongside them. When Cuauhtli joined the army, he had little more than a breech clout called a maxtlatl, sandals, and a short cape that his mother had woven for him. He was later taught from a pictographic book by his teachers what each uniform was called, how it was constructed, and what it signified.

Rank distinctions in uniform between warriors depended upon how many captives each individual had taken. A soldier trained in the telpochcalli who had captured two of the enemy was entitled to wear the cuextecatl, a trophy uniform derived from the military dress of the Huaxtecs in commemoration of their defeat under Motecuhzoma I. The outfit consisted of a tight-fitting body suit called a tlahuiztli, that was woven of cotton and to which were sewn red, yellow, blue, or green feathers. A conical hat in matching color was worn as well. A soldier who succeeded in capturing three of the enemy was awarded a long ichcahuipilli together with a back ornament shaped as a butterfly. A soldier who succeeded in capturing four of the enemy was awarded a

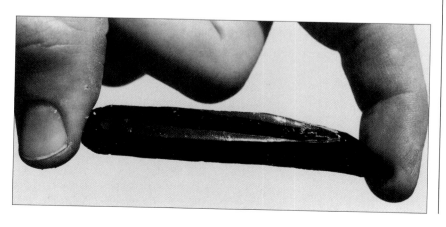

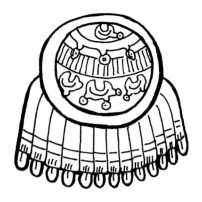

jaguar suit and helmet, and those who captured five of the enemy were awarded a green feather tlahuiztli and a back ornament called the xopilli or "claw". Accomplished soldiers who decided to become "lifers" were given a choice in promotion to a command position, or transfer to a troop of cuahchique, the "berserkers" of the Aztec Imperial army.

The priests of the calmecac were similarly rewarded. When attending to their duties at the temples, priests were sworn to poverty and required to wear a xicolli, a simple unadorned cotton jacket that tied at the front. On the battlefield they were rewarded with garments that were every bit as lavish as the warriors of the telpochcalli. Those who had captured two of the enemy were awarded a white tlahuiztli and a back ornament, in reality the ritual staff of the goddess Tlazolteotl. Three captives earned one the right to wear a green tlahuiztli and a pamitl or flag painted with red and white stripes topped by a panache of priceless green quetzal feathers. Priests who had captured four of the enemy were awarded a cuextecatl in black ornamented with white circles representing stars. A soldier who captured five of the enemy wore a red tlahuiztli with a back ornament consisting of a great fan of scarlet macaw feathers called a momoyactli. Those lucky enough to achieve six captures were awarded coyote uniforms of yellow or red feathers and wooden helmets.

Military rank was also dependent upon social structure. The great speaker or huey tlatoani sat at the apex of Aztec society. By the 15th century the position had become tantamount to emperor. Below the tlatoani was a class of petty-kings or princes called tetecuhtin (tecuhtli, sing.) drawn from the pipiltin (pilli, sing.) or lords. However, ambitious commoners called macehualtin (macehual, sing.) could attain princely rank through achievement in warfare if they survived. This was accomplished by promotion through a series of officer ranks of which we know the names of at least 10. In addition there were four commanding officers (doubtless more restricted to the pipiltin) called the tlacatecatl, the tlacochcalcatl, the huitznahuatl, and the ticocyahuacatl. Those who were promoted to the rank of captain and higher were awarded lavish uniforms equal to their high status, the most distinctive element being the large feather back ornaments that enabled them to be easily seen by their men as they walked up and down the back of the line shouting out their commands. Perhaps the most unusual outfit was that of the Tlacochcalcatl or Keeper of the House of Darts. These commanders were often close relatives of the emperor, in fact Itzcoatl and

By far the three most common shields awarded to Aztec soldiers were the cuexyo design (right), a cuexyo variant featuring water crescent pictographs (left) and the xicalcoliuhqui or greca design (center). (Author's illustration from *Codex Mendoza*

Motecuhzoma had served as Tlacochcalcatl before they were promoted to huey tlatoani. The uniform included a frightening helmet that represented a tzitzimitl or demon that was believed to take vicious revenge on all enemies.

When not wearing their battlefield gear, soldiers and officers alike were also entitled to wear a distinctive cloak called a tilmatli. The capes ranged in size from four to six feet (1.22–1.83m) in length and were customarily tied at the right shoulder and allowed to fall loosely over the body. Like the military uniforms themselves the tilmatli was ornamented in such a way that soldiers could be recognized for their accomplishments throughout the city: for example, a commoner who had captured one of the enemy was awarded a tilmatli ornamented with flowers, two captives earned the right to wear a tilmatli dyed orange with a striped border. Consequently, the higher he advanced in rank, the more elaborate a tilmatli he was entitled to wear. The richest were woven, dyed, hand painted, and embroidered with so much attention to detail that Europeans compared them to the finest garments of silk.

As Cuauhtli stood anxiously in the line, he was conscious of a towering object moving through the crowd of troops to his right. He soon recognized it as the emblem of an old war captain named Ocelotl. Ocelotl moved out from the ranks and turned to address the troops:

"In the words of the legendary Tlacaelel, I wish to give more courage to those of strong heart and embolden those who are weak. Know now that the Emperor has willed that the golden garlands, the featherwork, labrets, earrings, armbands, weapons, shields, insignia, rich cloaks, and breechcloths are not to be purchased in the market by brave men. Our sovereign delivers them personally as payment for memorable deeds. Upon returning from the war each of you will receive rewards according to his merits so that you can display proof of your worth to your families and your gods. If any of you should think to later 'borrow' such glory, remember that the only reward that awaits you is execution. So fight on, men, and earn your wealth and reputation here at this military marketplace!"(3)

The comparison to a market place was more than metaphorical. Cuauhtli knew that in ancient societies, much like the Mixtecs and Zapotecs of his own time, the production and consumption of luxury goods in cotton and feathers was restricted to the elite. Commoners like himself were even forbidden to wear jewelry. Royal women were the principal craft producers and so the kings sought to marry many wives not only because they could forge new alliances but because they could enrich themselves by exchanging their artistic creations through dowry, bridewealth, and other gift-giving networks. Considering that a king might marry as many as 20 times, each palace could produce luxury

A shield bearing the feather cuexyo design illustrating strips of leather added to the lower rim to protect the legs. This shield was reconstructed following the dimensions of the few surviving examples at 27.5 inches (70cm). Significantly the proportion of these shields to the human body was then found to be larger than what is portrayed in *Codex Mendoza*. The feather design was created using an adhesive, originally derived from plants of the orchid family. (Author's reconstruction)

goods to be measured in tonnage. By AD 1200, royal palaces throughout the central and southern highlands began to engage in fiercely competitive reciprocity systems in order to enhance their position in alliance networks. Many would be quick to perceive that the greater a royal house's ability to acquire exotic materials and to craft them into exquisite jewels, textiles, and featherwork, the better marriages it could negotiate. The better marriages it could negotiate, the higher the rank a royal house could achieve within a confederacy and in turn the better access it would have to more exotic

A helmet of carved hard wood, brilliantly painted to represent a ferocious jaguar. This example is executed in a traditional style of Mexican wood carving directly derived from Pre-Columbian antecedents. (Author's reconstruction)

materials, merchants, and crafts people. In short, royal marriages promoted syndicates.

The Aztec strategy through military conquest was to subvert the luxury economies of foreign states by forcing them to produce goods for their own unique system of gift exchange, rewards for military valor that made the soldiers of the imperial armies dependent upon the emperor himself for promotion in Aztec society. The outlandish uniforms seen on the battlefield therefore served as graphic proof of the kind of crushing tribute demands the Aztec empire could inflict as well. Surviving records tell us that no fewer than 50,000 cloaks a month were sent by the conquered provinces to Tenochtitlan. The prospect of being forced to subvert their artistic skills to the production of military uniforms that were then redistributed to an ever more glory-hungry army of princes and commoners alike must have been a frightening proposition if not an outright insult to those who would challenge the empire.

As Cuauhtli pondered the words of the old captain, he suddenly saw the cuahchique ahead of him beginning to turn and head back to the refuge of their comrades. Their insults had gotten the enemy so angry that their first rank had formed themselves up into a flying wedge to try to smash through the Aztec battleline. Cuauhtli was nervous but felt pretty sure of himself standing next to one of his cousins, a burly veteran wearing an impressive green feather otomi suit. The young soldier he had been assigned to serve was visibly shaken though. He could see the beads of sweat on the back of his pale neck. Suddenly a barrage of arrows and sling stones was shot into the air over Cuauhtli's head and showered down like black rain upon the enemy. Scores stumbled and fell into the long grass but the wedge hurled forward undaunted.

As the frightening war cries of the foe grew louder it appeared to Cuauhtli as if the spearhead of the wedge was heading right for him. He closed his eyes, gritted his teeth, and secured the tepoztopilli against his chest. Seconds later it felt as if every bone in his body was shattering from the impact as the Tlaxcalteca drove themselves through the line. Cuauhtli opened his eyes wide only to find himself staring into the face of the young soldier in front of him, screaming as he was dragged backwards by the hair into the enemy swarm. Cuauhtli struggled forward to help his comrade but soon found himself surrounded. He instinctively swung the butt of his weapon around and smashed one Tlaxcalan youth in the jaw knocking him unconscious. A second swung his macuahuitl at Cuauhtli's head, but Cuauhtli ducked. The soldier was about to catch him in the neck on the return stroke when suddenly his face went pale, he threw his shield into the air and ran off at the sight of Cuauhtli's cousin advancing forward with a hefty, five-foot (1.52m) long, two-handed macuahuitl of his own. Cuauhtli stood dumbfounded as he watched the veterans close in from the flanks to entrap those too late to flee for their lives. Then old Ocelotl called to the men at the back of the line: "Over here ... Cuauhtli's got his first captive!" Two youths especially assigned to the task immediately hurried forward with ropes, hog-tied the dazed man lying at Cuauhtli's feet, fastened a heavy wooden collar over his neck, and dragged him to the rear of the line. Cuauhtli had made his first capture and now he would stand with the veterans during the coming festival of Tlacaxipehualiztli and receive the flower cloak of a true warrior from the emperor's own hand.

In addition to distinctions in ritual dress, warriors were entitled to wear their hair in styles appropriate to their rank. The soldier on the left is wearing the more typical top-knot temilotl-style. The cuahchic on the right has shaved his head to form a central crest with two side tufts. (Author's illustration)

CAMPAIGN AND SUPPLY

In 1505, Cuauhtli was singing a song dedicated to the new emperor, Motecuhzoma Xocoyotzin, together with the other soldiers around a campfire in front of their tents and awnings of woven grass mats. After making his fourth capture he was proud to have earned the right to wear the nacazminqui, a black and yellow cloak with a red ornamental border. Life had been good ever since his first battlefield experience in the Atlixco Flower War. When he had turned 21 the previous month, Cuauhtli had started construction on a house for himself and his bride to live in within his father's compound. He hoped to have a son of his own when he returned home from this campaign against the Mixtecs of Tututepec. The rumor among the troops was that the empire had organized more than 400,000 men for the campaign. Many thought this was nothing but exaggeration, rumors spread in advance to intimidate the enemy. Cuauhtli took one of his wife's tortillas out of his bag and munched on it while he pondered how the supreme commanders could have organized such an army.

Although many scholars question the size of Aztec armies described in Spanish Colonial historical accounts, the fact was that such large armies were indeed feasible if for no other reason than the fact that the Aztecs could amass food and resources unmatched by any other civilization in the world. We assume that the inequalities between rulers and ruled, a condition of all early civilizations, first developed with the consolidation of social power by ancient tribal "big men": these dominated society by coordinating agricultural labor and supervising the storage and redistribution of crop surpluses, that insured group survival against drought. A plant ancestor of maize called teosinte may have first been nurtured in the wild by prehistoric shamans as "medicine" in the treatment of disease as early as 5000 BC. Eventually human selection encouraged the plant to evolve into a supplementary feasting food employed by individuals seeking to enhance their social status as paramount chiefs. Grains of incipient maize, for example, were too small to constitute a staple. Instead it was probably consumed as atole, an intoxicating brew that continues to be used as a celebratory drink throughout rural Mexico today. Once domesticated foods had been established as staples, however, they became available to any Pre-Columbian population interested in shifting from hunting and foraging to agriculture and sedentary life. Pre-Columbian agriculture allowed societies to increase their population, but this in turn created a demand for more intensive cultivation. The Aztecs met the challenge by developing a wide variety of agricultural techniques, from constructing terraces on mountain sides to digging hundreds of miles of canals and even creating artificial wetlands. Maize

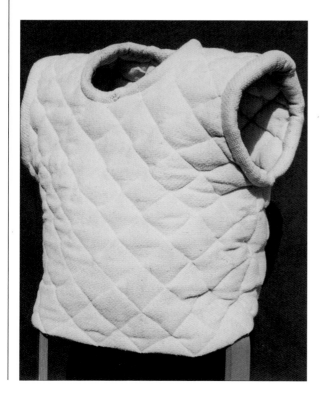

A simple cotton quilted armor jacket was the most basic warrior garment. Worn under the tlahuiztli or the ehuatl, it gave a soldier a formidably stout appearance. (Author's reconstruction)

Sahagún's *Primeros Memoriales* depicts an Aztec captain wearing an ehuatl or tunic of feathers sewn to a cotton backing. Although feathers were certainly employed to ornament the skirt for ritual dress, the author's reconstruction features heavy leather strips more conducive to battlefield conditions.

was the equivalent to wheat in Europe or rice in Asia. What made the Mesoamerican diet so spectacularly rich in protein, however, was the steady diet of maize together with beans and squash, nearly precluding the need for meat.

The only domesticated animals the Aztecs relied on were the dog and the turkey. Once the fields had been planted, the crops naturally lured deer and peccary (wild pigs) out of the wilderness so that hunters could kill the animals on the spot or capture them and keep them at home by tethering. In some areas people even kept deer and milked them like domestic animals. Women became the household scientists responsible for raising animals around the home and breeding and nurturing plants in nearby gardens. Men spent most of their time laboring in the fields. Nowhere in the world was so much energy invested in domesticating plants and we owe a debt of gratitude to the ancient Aztecs for creating what would eventually become the staples of our own dinner tables: corn, beans, squash, tomatoes and a host of other foods.

The Aztec army depended on two sources of supply, the calpulli itself and stores assembled by tributary kingdoms at designated points along the route of march. Much of the food that Cuauhtli was eating had been prepared by his own family or was contributed in tax by the market place vendors. This was to insure that the army caused as little impact on the

The highest percentage of warrior outfits demanded by the Aztec empire in tribute were the Huaxtec and jaguar style uniforms. Note the variant of the Huaxtec helmet complete with false wig and spindle whorls decorated with un-spun cotton commemorating a fertility goddess called Tlazolteotl. (Author's illustration from *Codex Mendoza*)

economies of allied nations as possible. Any serious devastation by an army to crops or the men and women who grew them was to be avoided under all circumstances. Cuauhtli's father might have been a craftsman but he was expected to put in his share of labor in the calpulli's communal fields as well. Once the harvest was reaped in October, the maize was husked, dried, and ground in the family compound with manos and metates of stone. The pulverized meal was then moistened with water, shaped in six-inch (15cm) round flat cakes, and toasted on a hot, flat ceramic disk. With the onset of the war season in November, Cuauhtli's mother, sisters, and wife shared responsibilities in preparing a host of tortillas, beans, chili peppers and other seasonings as well as jerky of dried venison, peccary, and turkey, all lovingly packed into a large basket to be carried by the telpochcalli boy who would serve Cuauhtli during the coming campaign. Then Cuauhtli's family withdrew to spend four days fasting and praying to the gods for his safety. Later his father would make daily penitential offerings by drawing blood with thorns from his tongue, ears, arms, and legs to insure that the gods brought his son home safely the following spring.

During the first long-distance campaigns, the Triple Alliance had to rely on porters called tlamemehque to transport the bulk of the provisions and equipment. No fewer than 100,000 had accompanied the troops that attacked Coixtlahuaca in 1458 with each carrying as much as 50 pounds in materiel. Later, as foreign kingdoms throughout southern and eastern Mexico were subjugated, the empire required that they maintain permanent stores to be used by the army when traveling through their territory. Consequently by 1500, the Aztecs would have ad little trouble maintaining armies in the hundreds of thousands in the field for years at a time if need be. The Mexica army was mobilized on the basis of units of 8,000 men called xiquipilli drawn from each of the 20 calpulli of Tenochtitlan. After each xiquipilli had been mobilized the huey tlatoani and his advisors had to determine how to most effectively move it out of the city. The solution was to space departure times over a period of several days so that the movement of the army would have the least impact on the ordinary business of the city. Once the army was outside, it probably averaged anywhere between 10 and 20 miles (16–32km) a day depending upon the urgency of a situation or the need to make a surprise assault. The sheer numbers of men involved in the march on Tututepec would have necessitated the need to designate different departure days for each xiquipilli. Considering that the Tenochtitlan army was then joined by an army of allies in equal numbers, no fewer than four different routes would have had to be taken, probably explaining the widely divergent pattern of battles recorded throughout southern Mexico during the course of the campaign. The need to divide large invasion armies suggests that the Aztecs were relying on something resembling the "Corps d'Armée" employed in 18th-and 19th-century Europe in which armies were divided into self-sufficient bodies of troops that moved *en masse* along separate but parallel routes toward a pre-determined destination. The tactical assumption was that each corps would be large enough to pin down any opposing army that got in its way until it could be joined by another. When an enemy had been fully engaged, the corps comm-ander would send runners out to alert the rest of the army who then endeavored to arrive at the scene of battle within hours and attack the enemy's exposed flanks or rear. Since all Aztec armies were com-posed of "light infantry", any corps could move fast when the situation de-manded making this strategy particularly effec-tive in even the most rugged terrain.

The coordination of such massive troop move-ments would have depended on a body of well-trained officers. How the chain of command actually functioned remains unknown however. The huey tlatoani was the

From left to right are an otomi rank suit with the xopilli or "claw" back device, a tlacatecatl captain's outfit with the quaxolotl back device, and a tlacochcalcatl captain's outfit with a tzitzimitl demon helmet. (Author's illustration from *Codex Mendoza*)

commander-in-chief and often took a personal role in field combat, especially during the early days of the empire. Second in command was the Cihuacoatl or Snake Woman, a position of paramount importance in the priesthood that was first attained by the Motecuhzoma's younger half-brother Tlacaelel and was subsequently passed on to his son and grandson. The Cihuacoatl was responsible for governing Tenochtitlan in the absence of the emperor, but could also act as commander-in-chief on the battlefield as well. Normally the supreme council of four commanders were directly responsible for the army during campaign. Each fulfilled a different role in terms of organizing supply lines, planning the routes of march, devising battlefield strategy, and directing the actual attack. There were officer ranks equivalent to those of major, colonel, captain and so forth that carried out the plans of the supreme council. As the son of a commoner, the highest rank Cuauhtli could hope to attain was that of a cuauhpilli, something like a commander with a knighthood but all the respect given a high-born lord.

Once supply lines from Tenochtitlan itself were overextended, the army had to rely on stores contributed by tributary city-states along the designated route of march. The Aztec empire was unique in that it did not attempt to secure vast amounts of territory but rather was more concerned with controlling strategic locations along primary routes of commercial exchange. Foreign noblemen placed in high office by the Aztecs became the most powerful in their realms but they were forever indebted to the empire to retain their thrones at tremendous expense to their people. For this reason the Aztecs eventually found it necessary to assign tax collectors to various kingdoms who were supported by permanent garrisons of Aztec troops. Following the conquest of Coixtlahuaca, the empire had devised a number of ingenious strategies for dividing up the confederacies of Eastern Nahua, Mixtec, and Zapotec city-states. Initial tactics were ruthless. Under Motecuhzoma I, defeated

Codex Mendoza **shows a priest burning copal incense in a ladle-like burner. Sworn to poverty, the novitiates wore a simple shirt-like garment called a xicolli that tied at the front. When fasting they left their hair unkempt and matted with blood from the penitential offerings they were expected to make by piercing their ears. (Right, author's illustration from** *Codex Mendoza***; center and left, author's reconstruction)**

The priest on the left has captured four of the enemy and has been awarded a variant of the Huaxtec uniform. The swirl of white dots on black signified a celestial constellation over a night sky. The priest on the right has captured five of the enemy and has been awarded a red feather tlahuiztli and back ornament together with a shield ornamented with an eagle's foot. (author's illustration from *Codex Mendoza*)

populations were either sold into slavery or brutally executed before the Great Temple of Tenochtitlan. The loss of valued labor was then replaced by Aztec populations who instituted new governments modeled on local prototypes. This was especially true of Huaxyacac (Oaxaca City) which even appointed its own king. In other cases, the Aztecs sought to maintain local political systems but subverted them by exploiting factional differences within royal families. We tend to think of ancient Mexican kingdoms as stable entities ruled over by omnipotent warlords who claimed divine rights to their thrones and married many times, not only to expand their alliance networks but also to increase their wealth. This practice however produced off-spring who, more frequently than not, disputed titles of inheritance and became embroiled in wars of succession that dissipated national cohesion. The Aztecs became masters at spotting weaknesses in foreign kingdoms and selecting their own candidates to support as claimants. Pictographic documents from Coixtlahuaca for example indicate that, following Atonal's death, an heir was appointed from a rival dynasty while one of Atonal's wives was appointed tax collector. In other cases, those desperate enough to "bargain with the devil" might actually invite the Aztec army into their territory in order to settle a dispute. On other occasions the disruption of political institutions could be helped along through more devious methods. Among the Eastern Nahua, Mixtecs, Zapotecs and their allies, royal marriages were often planned generations in advance. Once the Aztecs had conquered any single member of a confederation, the huey tlatoani or a ranking noble might demand a marriage with a local woman of royal blood. Such acts not only bound the Aztec royal line to that of the defeated but also disrupted predetermined marriage alliance patterns. No matter which strategy was employed the goal was to continually expand a network of foreign kings who could best support any Aztec army that needed to move through their territory in the course of a campaign.

So far things had run smoothly for Cuautli's xiquipilli. The men were well supplied through Acatlan, formerly an ally of Tututepec, but ever since the doomed reign of Tizoc, Mixtec kingdoms throughout the region had regularly engaged in both treachery and rebellion. Cuauhtli stood guard that night nervously listening to the howls of coyotes in the nearby hills. Suddenly he heard the sound of footsteps and challenged the intruder. Cuauhtli recognized the man and beckoned him forward. He was a famous merchant who had been leading trading expeditions to the Pacific coast for over 20 years; but had a reputation for being among the best of spies, even affecting disguises if need be. The merchant was cold, wet, and injured so he sat down by the fire. As Cuauhtli tended to his wounds he began to describe what had taken place in Tututepec. Motecuhzoma Xocoyotzin heard that the lapidaries of that city-state possessed a special sand with unique properties for polishing precious stones. He sent a party of 100 merchants to investigate. The merchants offered the lord of Tututepec fine cloaks, jewels, and precious featherwork as a gesture of goodwill. Believing the ambassadors to be spying for an Aztec invasion force, the lord of Tututepec had the merchants murdered and their bodies thrown into a river to conceal the evidence. This man had escaped by feigning death. Now Tututepec was fully aware of the location of Cuauhtli's division and the rest of the army. They had begun to erect massive fortifications of tamped earth in no fewer than five consecutive walls surrounding the city. All the main roads were blocked with tree trunks, rocks, and

Eagle warriors appear in stone sculpture and in some indigenous illustrations such as the *Lienzo de Tlaxcala*. Such uniforms were rare and apparently they were reserved for a special order of nobles. (Author's illustration)

Cuextecatl soldier with tepoztopilli (AD 1500)

A

Aztec battleline (AD 1500)

B

An invasion column divides (AD 1450)

The siege of Coixtlahuaca (AD 1458)

D

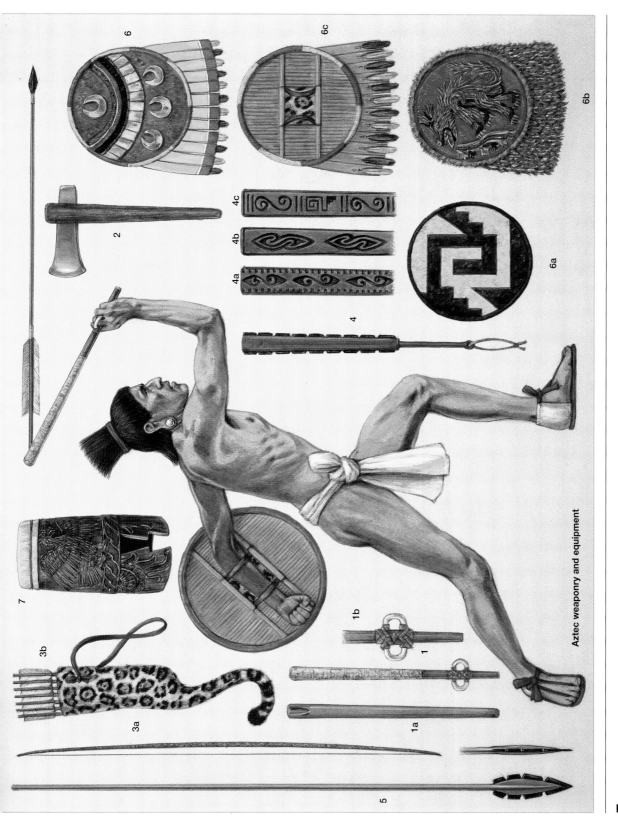

Aztec weaponry and equipment

E

Helmets and armor

Banners and flags

An Aztec squadron surprises the Huaxtecs (AD 1454)

H

Tlahuicol defends himself in gladiatorial combat before the Great Temple

The siege of Tenochtitlan (AD 1521)

J

brambles. The merchant got up, swilled the last of some hot cacao and promised Cuauhtli that he would cast a spell over the enemy in the morning that would destroy their spirit to fight. Cuauhtli took this remark very seriously. Sorcery was a critical element in Aztec warfare. It might appear to be little more than hocus pocus with magicians performing rituals and making burnt offerings before the onset of battle to invoke the gods to punish the enemy. The darker reality of their craft lay with use of plants like oleander from which they generated a poisonous smoke that caused severe nausea, vomiting, and even death when sent out on the wind. Contaminating food and water with disease was a slower but no less effective method for defeating an entrenched enemy who otherwise appeared impervious to siege. Palace curers even became killers when assassination was deemed necessary to resolve conflicts among royal family members. The merchant told Cuauhtli that the fastest way to the main temple and the royal palace was to head through the ballcourt north of the plaza. Then he politely asked for a share of the loot if the attack was successful, and disappeared back into the darkness.

Following their confirmation as tetecuhtin, all Aztec lords were entitled to wear the royal diadem or xihuitzolli composed of a mosaic of priceless turquoise tesserae affixed with adhesive to a wood or leather backing. (Author's reconstruction)

FIELD COMBAT

When the Aztec army arrived at Tututepec they were confronted with what appeared to be an impregnable position. The Pacific coast of Oaxaca was hot, desolate country overgrown by an impenetrable forest of low trees, brush, and cactus. Tututepec itself lay on the opposite side of a wide river swollen by early spring flooding. There the Mixtec army stood shouting insults in an effort to lure any who were foolhardy enough to try to swim for it. Motecuhzoma had now personally taken charge of the offensive. He immediately ordered his officers to locate trees of balsa wood from which to build a flotilla of rafts. Bridges for use at narrows further up river were constructed by weaving rope nets from vines and roots. Once these devices were completed the Aztecs planned a night-time crossing so that they would have the entire army assembled before the walls of Tututepec at daybreak. Cuauhtli was helped into his ornate red feather tlahuiztli by the youth assigned to serve him. He secured his jaguar helmet to his head, took up his macuahuitl, and joined an advance assault group at the river's edge.

The Aztecs were not usually concerned with positional war, or war for the possession of a defined battlefield area unless it served some particular purpose. Their goal was to maneuver the enemy into situations of entrapment and this demanded perfect coordination and timing. The first order of business was to raise a system of battlefield signals. This was achieved by establishing a command post on an adjacent hill with a direct sight line to the army. Signals were sent by relay. Runners were spaced out at two and a half mile (4km) intervals. Smoke was effective for communicating at longer distances between the xiquipilli, as were "heliographs" made from polished iron pyrite mirrors. When engaging in actual combat, however, commanders relied on the

A steward removes uniforms and weapons from a palace armory and displays them before Motecuhzoma II. (Author's illustration from the *Florentine Codex*)

enormous ornamental standards together with conch shell horns and drums. Lifting and waving was the principal means of getting the attention of the specific unit signified by a particular banner. Variance in the cadence of the musical instruments directed the unit into action. Field officers watched and listened for the messages. Once the battleline had extended itself, they then walked up and down the rear using whistles and to get their men's attention and barked out orders of attack or withdrawal depending on the progress of combat. Battles were generally opened with a good round of insults from both sides. For this reason the cuahchique were fond of wearing their hair in tufts much like professional clowns and even acted out skits mimicking the enemy's weaknesses in their efforts to get him to break ranks. The most obscene gestures of all imaginable kinds were especially popular and frequently involved exposing the buttocks and genitals. Even women and children were welcome to join in if the opportunity presented itself. Threats of extreme torture and cannibalism were considered especially inflammatory.

Hostilities generally opened with a mutual barrage of arrows, darts and sling bullets at 50 yards in an effort to disrupt formations. The Aztec employed bowmen and slingers from conquered provinces who could be deployed as mobile units either at the front of the line to instigate combat after which they retired to the rear, or directed to the flanks to lay down harassing fire. Frontline veterans were reliant on their superior armor and heavy, broad shields to withstand the rain of enemy projectiles; but sufficient injuries were soon inflicted among the youngest and most lightly armed troops, so that a charge would soon become a necessity. Aztec war was a running war. The vanguard depended on sheer inertia to try to smash through the enemy line and downhill attacks were considered optimal. The subsequent impact must have been horrific. Once troops on both sides had recovered, however, combatants would disperse widely into one-on-one engagements so that they could swing their deadly weapons unhindered. Slashing and parrying with the macuahuitl and shield demanded a tremendous expenditure of energy and so men were circulated every 15 minutes in order to keep the center strong. Officers kept a sharp eye out for any weaknesses in the enemy's formation and directed "flying" reserves of veterans to fill gaps among their own men as needed. Ultimately, the Aztecs preferred to surround their enemies and entrap them by double envelopment. This tactic could be dangerous as it necessitated extending the flanks at the expense of maintaining a strong center. The Aztecs off-set the problem by insuring that they had always fought with superior numbers. A surrounded and frightened enemy would fight to

In more traditional Mesoamerican societies like the Mixtecs and Zapotecs, the consumption of luxury goods was restricted to the elite who inherited their rights to rule by divine descent. Lesser ranking royal women and their children fulfilled the roles of principal craft producers and merchants for their royal palaces. The production capacity of a palace thereby became dependent upon how many women a lord could afford to marry and how well each was trained in fine art. (Author's illustration)

Son Merchant

Son Jeweler

GIFT

Second Wife

Third Wife

LADY

LORD

45

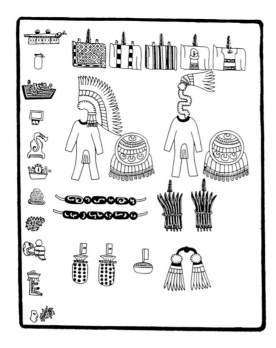

Above, a page from *Codex Mendoza* illustrates the tribute in gold, jade, feathers, and military uniforms collected each year from the principal Mixtec kingdoms of Oaxaca. Below, the *Florentine Codex* depicts Motecuhzoma II awarding jewels and clothing to two warriors. In this way the Aztecs subverted the production capacity of royal Mixtec palaces and the value of luxury goods in the elite economy. (Author's illustration)

the death if they thoug their lives were at stak Aztec commanders there fore tried to induc controlled retreats alon prescribed routes when panicked troops could I exposed to easy slaughte by reserves conceale in adjacent corn-field trenches, fox-holes, an even under piles of loos grass and leaves.

At day break, th Mixtecs awoke to find tha the Imperial army ha succeeded in fording th river during the night an teams of men were alread tearing into the lowe defensive wall with pick Soon Cuauhtli was runnin headlong up a scalin platform of bound can through a breach. On burly Mixtec prince shot a atlatl dart straight throug his shield coming with in inches of his ches Cuauhtli decapitated th man before he could eve draw his axe. As the Azte poured into the city, the found themselves embroi ed in a vicious street figh Then just as suddenly th enemy was nowhere to b found. Most appeared t have run off into the hill Acting on the advice of th merchant he had met the night before, Cuauhtli directed his squa through the ball court to where they spotted the famous House of Heaven dedicated to the Mixtec man-god Nine Wind. They dashed u the staircase and into the temple to seize the god's image and the sacre bundle containing his holy relics. Then they put the thatch of the roo to the torch to send a signal to Motecuhzoma and the supreme counc that the city had fallen.

Driven by the prospect of booty, the Aztec army had broken into disorganized mob but the victory celebration was short-lived. Little di they know that a second Mixtec army was already re-forming at anothe city to the north in hopes of encircling Tututepec themselves an trapping the Aztecs within the labyrinth of the streets and houses. Whe

Motecuhzoma was alerted of the danger by his spies, he issued orders for the Imperial troops to gather outside the city. Cuauhtli and his squad soon found themselves marching on the city of Quetzaltepec. When they arrived they immediately recognized that, unlike Tututepec, this would be no easy victory. The Mixtecs had amassed tons of stones, adobe, logs, and other debris upon the walls to cast down on the besiegers. That night the Mixtecs sang to the Aztecs in order to let them know that they were aware of their movements thereby frustrating any chance of a second surprise attack. When Motecuhzoma realized that the only resort was a prolonged siege the following morning, he addressed his men:

"Courageous Aztecs, Texcocans, Tepanecs, and all the men from the provinces: there is nothing we can do here but conquer or die. For this reason we have come. Our enemy shows valor and a brave heart and has decided to defend this city. I beg of you to demonstrate bravery in this endeavor. To die is to live in perpetual honor and glory." (Durán, 1994: 421–422)

While he was speaking, Mixtec troops began to form outside the walls. Their job was to "hit and run" harassing Imperial divisions who attempted to attack the walls directly and then just as quickly retreating into the surrounding formations of natural rock for protection. Motecuhzoma gave the order for the Aztecs, Chalcas, and Tlahuicas to move first. As Cuauhtli's xiquipilli advanced with scaling ladders they were soon beset by the Mixtecs from all sides. The fighting lasted all day. By sunset Cuauhtli had killed many men but he was badly wounded and exhausted. He was thankful when he heard that the Texcocans and Tepanecs, reportedly 100,000 strong, were to take the field in the morning. Their efforts were hardly more successful. After six days of almost continuous fighting, the Aztecs and their allies finally succeeded in taking the first line of Quetzaltepec's defenses. Fortifying themselves against attack from without they set about tunneling into the city. When a breach was finally made they waited until night and then poured into the city just as they had at Tututepec, burning and looting. But again the inhabitants had fled into the hills where they remained until a peace treaty was negotiated. The campaign had come to a draw. Cuauhtli had enriched himself in gold, turquoise, and other precious stones that he had plundered but there would no chance of taking any truly worthy captives from among the Mixtec princes back to Tenochtitlan that year.

Soldiers captured on the battlefield were immediately bound by hand and foot. Many were further incapacitated with heavy wooden collars through which three-foot (0.91m) long canes or wooden rods were secured with attached rings. (Author's illustration from Codex Mendoza)

BRINGING HOME THE WAR: AZTEC RELIGION AND RITUAL

In the years that followed the Tututepec campaign, the Tlaxcalteca had renewed their efforts to expand their sphere of control by fomenting trouble among disaffected city states throughout Puebla and northern Oaxaca. Campaigns continued to be waged against many Mixtec kingdoms as well as the Huexotzinca, Cholulteca, and their Eastern Nahua allies; always providing Cuauhtli with new opportunities to rise ever further up the ladder of military promotion. In 1519, the seasoned veteran stood with his sixth captive before the Great Temple. As he listened to the speeches given by the old generals he gazed around the plaza at the multitude of thousands who had come to witness the triumph of that day. His own family was there. His father and uncles were beaming with pride. His mother knew that she would live out her years in real comfort after a life of toil. But, Cuauhtli's wife was concerned if he would choose to take a promotion with the officer corps, as she hoped, or whether he would dedicate himself to that elite regiment sworn to eternal combat, the dreaded cuahchique.

As Cuauhtli got a firmer grip on the hair of his terrified prisoner kneeling at his feet he looked upon the shrine of Huitzilopochtli and pondered the story of the god to whom he was to pay his debt. In a time long ago there lived a woman named Coatlicue, Lady Serpent Skirt, together with her 400 sons. The woman always performed her penance dutifully sweeping on Snake Mountain near the ancient Toltec city of Tollan. One day as she was attending to her chores she gathered up a ball of feathers, placed them at her waist, and miraculously conceived another child. When her 400 sons saw that their mother was pregnant they were enraged. Their sister Coyolxauhqui arrived and addressed them all saying:

> "My elder brothers, she has dishonored us, we can only kill our mother, the wicked one who is now with child."

At first Coatlicue was terrified at what her children were plotting. Then just as suddenly a young warrior sprang forth from her womb fully armed. Huitzilopochtli stood atop Coatepec ready to defend his mother against the coming onslaught. Coyolxauhqui dashed to the top of the hill but Huitzilopochtli struck her down with a mighty blow from his spear thrower and lopped off her head. Her body twisted and turned as it fell to the ground at the foot of

Musicians such as these were stationed with a signal banner corps to relay messages across the battlefield. A teponaztli, a huehuetl, and a conch shell trumpet are featured. (Author's illustration from the *Florentine Codex*)

48

A popular instrument among many ancient civilizations, the conch was capable of issuing a modulated, bellowing sound that could be heard for miles.

the mountain. Huitzilopochtli cast down the 400 brothers in equal measure, slew them, and took their raiment as warriors for himself in commemoration of his conquest.

It was the sworn duty of each and every Aztec soldier to carry on the legacy of the great patriarch Huitzilopochtli, the Hummingbird of the South; to be ever vigilant, ever prepared to protect his family, his calpulli, and his city from those who would destroy all that his ancestors had worked so hard to accomplish. By now the captive had resigned himself to his fate. He knew the fortunes of war when he joined his own army. "Cuauhtli, now I go where I will wait for you. I go proudly and they will sing of me in my homeland" he said. Cuauhtli whispered in response: "Today you … tomorrow me." Then the priests approached and Cuauhtli made the presentation: "Here is my well beloved son," and the captive responded: "Here is my revered father." Now was the time for the final conflict, the triumph, the conclusion of battle to be personally witnessed there in the central precinct by all the Aztec people. Every captive walking up those stairs that day represented the hated siblings who in their jealousy would have slain Huitzilopochtli. Each would reenact the role of the cosmic enemy, living proof of the god's omnipotent power manifest in the abilities of his spiritual descendants, his mighty warriors, to repay him for his blessings, indeed the very livelihood that they enjoyed. When Cuauhtli's captive reached the top of the stairs, he was stretched out on his back over a stone and held down by four priests. Then a fifth priest drove a knife into the captive's chest, the trauma of the blow killing him nearly instantaneously. Just as quickly the priest slit the arteries of the heart and lifting the bloody mass into the air pronounced it to be the "precious eagle cactus fruit"; the supreme offering to the Sun god Tonatiuh. The heart was then burned in a special vessel carved in the shape of an eagle. The lifeless corpse of the captive was tossed down the staircase where it came to rest next to the stone image of the decapitated goddess Coyolxauhqui.

Among more ancient Mesoamerican societies like the Mayas, Mixtecs, and Zapotecs, war was the province of elite factions, close relatives and kin, that seized each other's lands and property by presenting rival claims of legitimacy through descent from divine ancestors. It was not enough to simply kill an enemy in a remote field. Successful usurpers had to display their captives before assembled lineage members, to dispatch their enemies in accordance with their exalted positions as divine rulers, and to demonstrate publicly the institution of a new social order. In today's world we witness war on television to confirm for ourselves that what our government claims it is doing to ensure our national security is worth the cost in resources and

Merchants operating out of their headquarters in Tlatelolco served as the vanguard of Aztec expansionism. Prosperous as they were, they were permitted to travel virtually anywhere in Mesoamerica where they traded for goods such as exotic parrot feathers from Veracruz or gold and gems from Oaxaca. Merchants even functioned as spies going so far as to affect accents, learn foreign languages, and create disguises to investigate kingdoms on which they sought to make war. (Author's illustration from the *Florentine Codex*)

human life. Ancient societies had no comparable way to convey the image of battle, so heads of state devised ways of re-creating event through festivals in order to foster public trust. Nowhere did the practice find greater expression than among the Aztecs.

Thousands of Aztec people participated in these events, reassuring themselves that their investment in supplying food, making weapons and equipment, and committing the lives of their children would grant them the benefits of conquest that their emperors guaranteed. Warfare, human sacrifice, and the promotion of agricultural fertility were inextricabl linked in religious ideology. Aztec songs and stories describe how the sun was created through the self-sacrifice of a god. But the sun god refused to move through the sky without an offering of something equal to his own gift. He therefore demanded nourishment in the form of human hearts and blood. The people invented war to feed the sun his holy food and thereby perpetuate life on earth. The Aztecs didn't use the term human sacrifice nor did they consider their ritual activities in any way connected to such a practice as it was later cast on them by Europeans. For them it was nextlaualli – sacred debt payment to the gods.

Cuauhtli stood in the patio of his family's compound greeting guests as they came to compliment him on his promotion to the cuauhpipiltin. His high status not only freed him from all tribute obligations to the state, but even insured a place for his son in the ranks of the Aztec nobility. As Cuauhtli stared at the boy playing in the garden with the other children, he realized that he could now afford to send him to the calmecac to be educated as a scholar. He was relieved when he thought of the numerous times that he had almost been slain, captured, or lay badly wounded in some remote field in a far distant land. But there was a darker side to his son's future. Shortly before he died, Nezahualpilli, the son of Nezahualcoyotl and Tlatoani of Texcoco, prophesied an end to the empire, telling Motecuhzoma:

> "You must be on guard, you must be warned, because I have discovered that in a very few years our cities will be ravaged and destroyed. We and our children will be killed, our subjects humbled. Of all these things you must not doubt. Before many days have passed you will see signs in the sky that will appear as an omen of what I am saying." (Durán, 1994: 452)

The Aztec people began to see the signs of catastrophe everywhere. In 1517, a tongue of flame rose in the east and pointed into the heavens like

Merchants provided the Aztec emperor and his war council with detailed paintings for military logistics. Here a map is presented to two tetecuhtin or high-ranking lords describing how the defenses of a city, appearing in the upper right-hand corner, can best be penetrated. (Author's illustration from the *Florentine Codex*)

An enemy generally admitted defeat when the Aztec army succeeded in burning the temple of a town's principal god. Note the Huexotzincan warrior covering his mouth in astonishment as a warrior torches the temple. (Author's illustration from the *Florentine Codex*)

a dagger. Then the Temple of Huitzilopochtli mysteriously burned. A comet appeared in broad daylight hurtling through the sky like a spear of fire. Then the waters of Lake Texcoco began to turn and boil and threatened to burn houses along the lake shore. Some people even reported seeing two-headed monsters in the streets of the city, but Cuauhtli knew that often such stories were made up by disaffected individuals, perhaps some prince who had been stripped of his title in disgrace who hoped to overthrow the government himself. But in 1519, there was news of the arrival of strangers from the east. They dressed themselves in clothing of silver metal and rode to war on the backs of giant deer. Before long, word reached Motecuhzoma that first the Totonacs and then the Tlaxcaltecs had declared the leader of this bizarre enemy to be nothing less than the great god Quetzalcoatl, now returned to reclaim his kingdom from his mortal enemies, Tezcatlipoca and Huitzilopochtli. There were always prophecies of doom but this one was to be considered a serious threat. The Eastern Nahuas, Mixtecs, and Zapotecs all revered the Plumed Serpent as their patron god. Their kings and queens were even accustomed to calling themselves the "Children of Quetzalcoatl". The prophecy of his return in the Aztec year One Reed would be taken as nothing less than a call to abandon their petty disputes and to rise up together as independent nations to overthrow the yoke of Aztec imperialism forever.

In reality, there were hundreds of Cuauhtlis in Aztec society, each destined to fight to the death in defense of the empire as it had been predetermined by the calpulli's tonalpouqui according to the date of a child's birth. We can only imagine what became of each of these highly trained and fearsome individuals in their war against the Spaniards and their Indian allies. Many would fall at the battle of Otumba fighting valiantly with the Cihuacoatl. Others would defend Tenochtitlan to the man with Cuauhtemoc, the valiant last emperor of the once omnipotent Aztec Empire of the Triple Alliance.

Proud of itself
is the city of Mexico-Tenochtitlan
Here no one fears to die in war
This is our glory
This is your command
oh Giver of Life!
Have this in mind, oh princes,
do not forget it.
Who could conquer Tenochtitlan?
Who could shake the foundation of heaven?(4)

(Below left) A colossal statue depicts the decapitated mother of Huitzilopochtli, Coatlicue. The dual snake heads signify blood gushing from the wound (Author's illustration). (Below right) Huitzilopochtli appears atop Coatepec or Snake Mountain dismembering his sister Coyolxauhqui and her four hundred brothers in the *Florentine Codex*. The religious story was a fusion of history, legend, and cosmic allegory in which the Aztec hero representing the sun each day struck down the moon, the lady of the night. (Author's illustration from the *Florentine Codex*)

NOTES

1) Adapted from Sahagún 1950–1982, Book 6: 171–172, 179, Book 4: 38–39.
2) In earlier publications I referred to the Eastern Nahua as the Aztec-Chichimecs or Tolteca-Chichimeca to distinguish them from the Aztecs of the Basin of Mexico (Pohl 1991). Historian James Lockart (1992) advocates Eastern Nahua and I have found it a useful term.
3) Adapted from a speech attributed to Tlacaelel cited by Durán 1994: 234.
4) Aztec poem translated from the Nahuatl by Léon-Portilla 1969: 87.

BIBLIOGRAPHY

Anawalt, Patricia Rieff
   1977   What Price Aztec Pageantry? *Archaeology*. Vol. 30 (4),
          pp. 226–233.
   1981   *Indian Clothing Before Cortés: Mesoamerican Costumes from the
          Codices*. Norman: University of Oklahoma Press.
   1982   Understanding Aztec Human Sacrifice. *Archaeology*. Vol. 35 (5),
          pp. 38–45.
   1993   Riddle of the Aztec Royal Robe. *Archaeology*. Vol. 46 (3),
          pp. 30–36.
Berdan, Frances F. and Patricia Rieff Anawalt
   1992   *Codex Mendoza*. Four Volumes. Berkeley: University of California
          Press.
Boone, Elizabeth Hill
   1994   *The Aztec World*. Montreal: St. Remy Press. Washington D.C.
          Smithsonian Books.
Broda, Johanna, Davíd Carrasco and Eduardo Matos Moctezuma
   1987   *The Great Temple of Tenochtitlan: Center and periphery in the Aztec
          World*. Berkeley: University of California Press.
Brumfiel, Elizabeth M.
   1987   Elite and Utilitarian Crafts in the Aztec State. In: *Specialization,
          Exchange and Complex Societies*. Edited by Elizabeth M. Brumfiel
          and Timothy K. Earle: pp. 102–118. Cambridge: Cambridge
          University Press.
Carrasco, Davíd and Eduardo Matos Moctezuma
   1992   *Moctezuma's Mexico: Visions of the Aztec World*. Niwot: University of
          Colorado Press.
Carrasco, Pedro
   1971   Social Organization of Ancient Mexico. In: *Handbook of Middle
          American Indians*. Vol. 10: 349–375. Edited by Gordon Ekholm
          and Ignacio Bernal. Austin: University of Texas Press.
Caso, Alfonso
   1978   *The Aztecs, People of the Sun*. Fifth Edition. Norman: University of
          Oklahoma Press.

A seven-inch (17.8cm) long obsidian knife blade. (Private collection)

Clendinnen, Inga
  1991   *Aztecs: An Interpretation.* Cambridge: Cambridge University Press.
Davies, Nigel
  1980   *The Aztecs, A History.* Norman: University of Oklahoma Press.
Durán, Diego
  1994   *The History of the Natives of New Spain.* Translated, Annotated, and with an Introduction by Doris Heyden. Norman: University of Oklahoma Press.
Fagan, Brian
  1984   *The Aztecs.* New York: W.H. Freeman and Co.
de Fuentes, Patricia
  1993   *The Conquistadors: First Person Accounts of the Conquest of Mexico.* Norman: University of Oklahoma Press.
Florescano, Enrique
  1993   *El Mito de Quetzalcóatl.* México: Fondo de Cultura Económica.
Gillespie, Susan D.
  1989   *The Aztec Kings: The Construction of Rulership in Mexica History.* Tucson: University of Arizona Press.
Hassig, Ross
  1988   *Aztec Warfare, Imperial Expansion and Political Control.* Norman: University of Oklahoma Press.
  1992   *War and Society in Ancient Mesoamerica.* Berkeley: University of California Press.
Heath, Ian
  1999   *Armies of the Sixteenth Century. Volume 2: The Armies of the Aztec and Inca Empires, Other Native Peoples of the Americas, and the Conquistadores, 1450–1608.* Guernsey, Great Britain: Foundry Books.
Klein, Cecelia
  1987   The Ideology of Autosacrifice at the Templo Mayor. In: *The Aztec Templo Mayor.* Edited by Elizabeth H. Boone, pp. 293–370. Washington D.C.: Dumbarton Oaks.
Léon-Portilla, Miguel
  1969   *Pre-Columbian Literatures of Mexico.* Norman: University of Oklahoma Press.
Lockhart, James
  1992   *The Nahuas after the Conquest: A Social and Cultural History of the Indians of Central Mexico, Sixteenth through Eighteenth Centuries.* Stanford: Stanford University Press.

Matos Moctezuma, Eduardo
  1988   *The Great Temple of the Aztecs: Treasures of Tenochtitlan.* London: Thames and Hudson.
Nicholson, H.B.
  1971   Religion in Pre-Hispanic Central Mexico. In: *Handbook of Middle American Indians.* Vol. 10: 395–446. Edited by Gordon Ekholm and Ignacio Bernal. Austin: University of Texas Press.
  2001   *Topiltzin Quetzalcoatl of Tollan: a Problem in Mesoamerican Ethnohistory.* Boulder: University of Colorado Press.
Nicholson, H.B. with Eloise Quinones Keber
  1983   *Art of Aztec Mexico: Treasures of Tenochtitlan.* Washington, D.C.: National Gallery of Art.
Pasztory, Esther
  1983   *Aztec Art.* New York: Harry N. Abrams Inc.
Pohl, John M.D.
  1991   *Aztec, Mixtec, and Zapotec Armies.* First Edition. Oxford: Osprey Publishing Ltd.
  1999   *Exploring Mesoamerica.* Oxford: Oxford University Press.
Quiñones Keber, Eloise
  1995   *Codex Telleriano Remensis.* Austin: University of Texas Press.
Sahagún, Bernardino de
  1950–1982 *Florentine Codex: General History of the Things of New Spain.* Translated from the Aztec into English by Arthur J. O. Anderson and Charles E. Dibble. Santa Fe: The School for American Research and the University of Utah.
  1993–1997 *Primeros Memoriales.* Two Volumes. Photography by Ferdinand Anders. Paleography of Nahuatl Text and English Translation by Thelma D. Sullivan. Completed and Revised with Additions by H.B. Nicholson, Arthur J.O. Anderson, Charles E. Dibble, Eloise Quiñones Keber and Wayne Ruwet.
Smith, Michael E.
  1994   *The Aztecs.* Blackwell Publishers.
Soustelle, Jacques
  1962   *The Daily Life of the Aztecs on the Eve of the Spanish Conquest.* New York: The Macmillan Company.
Stewart, Gene S.
  1981   *The Mighty Aztecs.* Washington D.C.: The National Geographic Society.
Townsend, Richard
  1992   *The Aztecs.* London: Thames & Hudson.

GLOSSARY

atlatl (ot-la-t) = spear-thrower

Aztec = "People of Aztlan" or Place of the Heron, collective name for the Nahuatl-speaking peoples of the Basin of Mexico

calmecac (call-may-cock) = priest's school

Camaxtli (ca-mosh-tlee) = name for Mixcoatl, father of Quetzalcoatl of legend

chinampa (chee-nom-pa) = an island field for planting

Coixtlahuaca (co-eesh-tla-waca) = Mixtec-Chocho kingdom of Oaxaca

cuahchic (kwa-cheek) = special warrior rank

Cuauhtli (co-wow-tlee) = person named for 15th of the 20 day signs of the sacred calendar

cuextecatl (kway-sh-tay-cot) = special warrior rank

ehuatl (ay-what) = battle tunic worn by noblemen

ichcahuipilli (each-ca-we-pee-lee) = cotton quilted armor

Huaxtec (wash-tek) = Indian people of northern Veracruz

huey tlatoani (way-tla-toe-oni) = great speaker, i.e. the Aztec emperor

Huitzilopochtli (wheat-zeeloh-poch-tlee) = Hummingbird of the South, patron god of the Aztecs

macehual (maa-say-wall) = peasant

macuahuitl (ma-kwa-wheat) = sword

Mexica (May-shee-ca) = the Aztec tribe that settled Tenochtitlan

Mixcoatl (meesh-co-ot) = Cloud Snake, Chichimec father of Quetzalcoatl, patron god of Tlaxaca and Huexotzinco

Mixtec (Meesh-tec) = Indian people of northern and western Oaxaca

Motecuhzoma (moe-tay-coo-zoh-ma) = name for two famous Aztec emperors

Nahua (na-wa) = population of Indian people living throughout central Mexico, the Aztecs were a branch of the Nahuas

Nahuatl (na-wa-t) = language of the Nahuas

Nezahualcoyotl (nez-who-all-coy-oat): famous tlatoani of Texcoco

nextlaualli (nesh-tla-wally) = debt-paying, Aztec term for sacrifice

Quetzalcoatl (Kate-zahl-co-ot) = Toltec culture hero of kingdoms throughout central and southern Mexico

Tarascan (tar-ass-can) = Indian people of Michoacan, more properly known as Purepecha

Tenochtitlan (ten-ohch-teet-lon) = capital city of the Mexica Aztec

tepoztopilli (tay-pose-toe-pee-lee) = halberd

tecuhtli (tay-coot-lee) = land-owning lord

telpochcalli (tell-poch-ca-lee) = young men's house-warrior school

tilmatli (till-mot-lee) = cape

tlatoani (tla-toe-oni) = "speaker", high ranking tecuhtli

tzitzimitl (see-see-meet) = demon

tonalpouqui (toe-nal-poo-key) = soothsayer

xiquipilli (she-quee-pee-lee) = unit of 8,000 men

Zapotec = Indian people of Oaxaca

The *Florentine Codex* depicts the execution of war captives whose hearts were torn from their bodies and offered to the sun. (Author's illustration)

COLOR ILLUSTRATIONS

PLATE A: CUEXTECATL SOLDIER WITH TEPOZTOPILLI (AD 1500)

Soldiers who succeeded in capturing two enemies were awarded a uniform consisting of a body suit called a tlahuiztli, a tall conical cap called a copilli, and a shield marked with black designs described as "hawk scratches". The tlahuiztli was made of sewn cotton. Red, yellow, blue or green feathers were meticulously stitched to the cloth in the workshops of conquered city-states and sent to Tenochtitlan each year as tribute. The design of the cap (1) was adopted as a trophy emblem from the Huaxtecs of coastal Veracruz following Motecuhzoma Ilhuicamina's subjugation of the region between 1469 and 1481. The frame was constructed of cane. The Huaxtec area held a particular fascination for the Aztecs because it was rich in cotton. The goddess of spinners and weavers was called Tlazolteotl. For this reason the soldiers thought it appropriate to wear hanks of un-spun cotton through their ear spools (2) as well as the yacameztli or "nose moon" in gold (3) in honor of her role as a patron of the moon. In addition to the battle suit, the emperor rewarded soldiers with a distinctive cape called a tilmatli that allowed them to display their rank when off-duty as well (4). The loin cloth or maxtlatl (5) was hand woven and embroidered by the soldier's own wife or mother (5a). The method of wrapping the cloth around the body and tying the ends at the front was a distinctive fashion for Aztec men (5b). The knot was then passed through an opening in the tlahuiztli. Sandals (6) were woven with thick grass soles to which were stitched a cotton strip to support the ankle and ties. Traditionally uniforms were burned upon the pyres of their owners at death, but during Spanish Colonial times the Indian descendants of great warriors continued to preserve the garments as valued objects of inheritance and even entitlement.

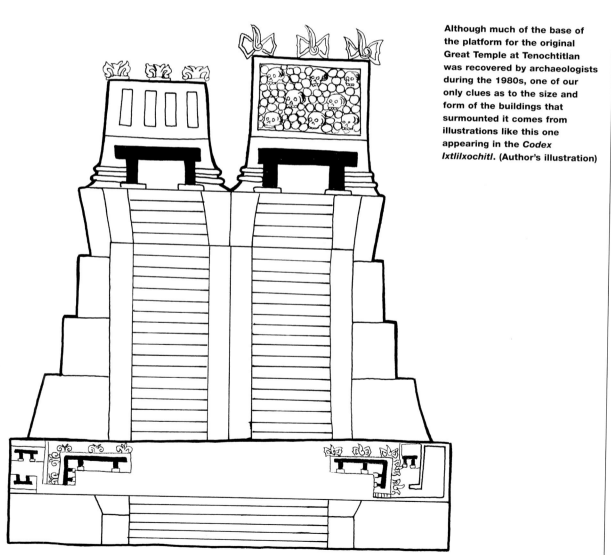

Although much of the base of the platform for the original Great Temple at Tenochtitlan was recovered by archaeologists during the 1980s, one of our only clues as to the size and form of the buildings that surmounted it comes from illustrations like this one appearing in the *Codex Ixtlilxochitl*. (Author's illustration)

PLATE B: AZTEC BATTLELINE (AD 1500)

Two cuahchique stand forward shouting insults and mocking the enemy in an effort to provoke the foolhardy to break ranks and attack the center of their main body. The Aztecs favored the deployment of troops in extended battlelines in their efforts to entrap their foes through double envelopment. The seemingly haphazard display of military pageantry is due to the fact that soldiers of differing ranks have been purposefully teamed up so that recruits can hone their skills in actual combat with the more experienced veterans. Having proven themselves competent fighters and eager to earn even greater rewards, the majority of front-line soldiers are of cuextecatl rank. They are easily identifiable by the cone-shaped copilli headdress. Soldiers of the more advanced jaguar and otomi ranks have moved forward through the mass of raw recruits gathered at the rear to prepare for the shock of an impending attack. The magnificent standard rising up over the back of the battleline signals the arrival of a captain who will evaluate the likelihood of an attack and relay the message to the supreme commanders who would be observing the situation from an adjacent promontory.

PLATE C: AN INVASION COLUMN DIVIDES (AD 1450)

Following the defeat of an Eastern Nahua city-state, Nezahualcoyotl explains to a Mexica Tlacochcalcatl the need for dividing troops into two columns of march. The strategy was intended to conserve local agricultural resources by reducing the consumptive impact of armies that could range upwards of 50,000 men. Nezahualcoyotl whose name meant "Fasting Coyote" was forced into exile as a youth after the assassination of his father Ixtlilxochitl by the hated Tepanec despot Tezozomoc. He later succeeded in formulating an alliance with the Mexica under Itzcoatl and together the two tlatoque destroyed the Tepanec capital of Azcapotzalco. The uniform of the Tlacochcalcatl is based on a plate from *Codex Mendoza*. Nezahualcoyotl's outfit comes from an illustration appearing in *Codex Ixtlilxochitl*. He wears

an ehuatl or tunic ornamented with rare tropical bird feathers. Coyote ears affixed to his wooden helmet and tipped with the paper banners of a penitent symbolize his name. The small huehuetl drum slung over his back was used to personally issue battlefield commands. High lords and others who could afford them wore greaves of metal. Soldiers on the march wore relatively simple clothing. Ranking warriors proudly displayed the capes given to them by the emperor's own hand. The young men assigned to them for training were responsible for packing basic supplies and carrying extra armaments.

One of the very few Aztec pyramids with a temple that could be restored accurately by archaeologists is preserved at Santa Cecelia Acatitlan in Mexico City. Such pyramids were located at the center of every community and served as a last refuge for defense. (Author's photograph)

PLATE D: THE SIEGE OF COIXTLAHUACA (AD 1458)

Lord Atonal battles Aztec squadrons employing broad, light-weight scaling-frames of bound cane or timber. The king himself wears the turquoise crown of a Toltec tecuhtli as well as a long xicolli favored by Mixtec noblemen. The prince with whom he is defending the ramparts is a Chocho ally who wears a crown of woven fiber and a special short ichcahuipilli of quilted cotton. The former is based on an image from the Lienzo Seler II while the latter appears in the Selden Roll. Both manuscripts are pictorial histories attributed to Coixtlahuaca artists. Between 1300 and 1450, Coixtlahuaca had become one of the richest kingdoms in Mesoamerica by controlling the principal trade routes that linked the Central Mexican Highlands with Veracruz, Oaxaca, and Chiapas. Every year merchants from all over Mesoamerica attended this kingdom's great market to trade in gold, turquoise, tropical bird feathers, cacao, scarlet cochineal dye, and even a special fabric made from woven rabbit hair. Lord Atonal wielded tremendous political power by negotiating alliances between the Mixtecs, the Chocho-Popoloca, the Eastern Nahua, and half-a-dozen other ethnic groups that occupied the region. Searching for an excuse to dismantle this ancient confederacy, the Aztecs accused Atonal of assassinating a hundred and sixty of their merchants. Motecuhzoma I and Nezahualcoyotl then organized an army of 300,000 men of whom no fewer than 100,000 served as porters for what would become the Triple Alliance's first long-distance campaign. Atonal fought valiantly but the Aztec host soundly defeated him before his allies could come to his aid. The doomed king was garroted and many of his men were executed in rituals before the Great Temple at Tenochtitlan.

PLATE E: AZTEC WEAPONRY AND EQUIPMENT

Being largely an army of light infantry, the Aztecs maintained a relatively limited arsenal of offensive weapons in comparison to other armies throughout the world. The most ancient were the spear thrower (1) and the axe (2). Early spear throwers were composed of little more than a stick carved with a trough and a hook to secure the shaft (1a). More sophisticated versions featured special loops for the forefingers (1b). It became a most effective weapon for medium-range combat in the hands of noble warriors specially trained in its use. Being essential to agricultural production, most prehistoric farmers fought for their tribal chiefs with axes of ground stone. The widespread adoption of metallurgical technology from South America after AD 900 fostered the development of the more vicious cast copper axe head as a special weapon. The bow (3a) and arrows (3b) were adopted rather late as hunting tools in Mesoamerica, but in the hands of the Aztec's Chichimec ancestors they soon became fundamental to laying down a barrage of deadly fire prior to an attack in warfare. The macuahuitl or sword (4) had been employed by earlier Mesoamerican civilizations. The Aztecs valued its particular ability to maim an enemy and were the first to employ it as a general issue

weapon. Many were carved or painted with intricate designs (4a–c).

While front-rank warriors engaged in slashing matches with the macuahuitl, troops armed with the tepoztopilli or halberd (5) harassed an enemy by thrusting or stabbing from the rear of the line. All Aztec soldiers were armed with shields. The few examples that survive in collections both in Mexico and Europe are all approximately thirty inches (76cm) in diameter (6). Most are parade shields featuring remarkable heraldic designs in feathers such as the stepped fret (6a) based on an example preserved in the Württembergisches Landesmuseum, Stuttgart, Germany, and a singing coyote (6b) preserved in the Museum für Volkerkunde, Vienna, Austria. The cuexyo shield (6c) is reconstructed from eyewitness accounts which describe battle shields as being constructed of resilient woven cane or bamboo with heavy double cotton backing. Drums (7) were essential to coordinating the movements of large units closing in for the kill. The example illustrated is based on a huehuetl preserved in Mexico's National Museum of Anthropology. It is three feet (0.91m) high and features a scene carved in relief depicting a dance of eagles and jaguars.

The Aztec emperors commissioned sculptures and erected them in and around the temples of the central precinct of Tenochtitlan to contextualize the architecture with images from religious stories. Over succeeding centuries many of these works were rediscovered in the course of excavations throughout Mexico City. This 19th-century lantern slide of the original museum at Casa de Moneda (1866-1964) depicts several famous carvings including a three-foot (0.91m) high jaguar cuauxicalli in which the hearts of executed prisoners were burned as offerings to the gods. The colossal diorite portrait in the center is that of Huitzilopochtli's sister Coyolxauhqui. Just behind the head of the moon goddess is the Stone of Tizoc that was employed for gladiatorial rituals. (Private collection)

PLATE F: HELMETS AND ARMOR

Nearly all warriors were issued with some form of the ichcahuipilli (1 and 2). The most basic form of this cotton quilted armor was a pull-over shirt. It was always worn under both the tlahuiztli and the ehuatl and gave the soldier a very muscular appearance. Other examples appearing in pictographic histories suggest that it was also worn as a tunic or jacket by itself among high ranking lords. Many were dyed in vibrant hues of red and blue. The ichcahuipilli was perfectly adapted to the hot humid climate that pervades much of Mexico. The theory behind its use was more like a contemporary bullet-proof vest for absorbing the blow of a weapon rather than attempting to stop it like medieval metal armor. Helmets were carved of hardwoods like mahogany. They were lined with a heavy cotton cap and tied securely under the chin with cloth or leather ribbons. Those issued as awards to soldiers were limited almost exclusively to the jaguar (3), coyote (4), and tzitzimitl (5) or "demon of vengeance" styles. However, high ranking nobility could commission helmets for themselves in all sorts of fanciful heraldic forms with eagles, parrots, vultures, monkeys, bears, wolves, and crocodiles being especially popular.

PLATE G: BANNERS AND FLAGS

The large ornaments or banners secured to the shoulders and backs of high ranking soldiers and officers were essential to coordinating troop movements. They had to be fairly light weight so they were created by artisans from wicker covered in cloth sewn with hundreds of feathers. According to *Codex Mendoza*, the quaxolotl banner (1) was umbrella-like in shape and was produced in yellow, blue, and green. The top was ornamented with the head of a dog called Xolotl whose ears had been ripped off according to a legend. The tlecocomoctli banner (2) was supposed to represent a headdress ignited by fire. This example appears in Sahagún's *Primeros Memoriales*. The banner worn by the huiznahuatl captain whose name meant "thorn speech" is a variation of the most basic signal flag or pamitl (3). The chimallaviztli or "shield insignia" featured the face of a grinning demon (4). The papalotl insignia (5) was meant to represent a butterfly. The caquatonatiuh meant literally the black and yellow troupial feather sun insignia (6).

Nowhere was the strategic significance of such banners more graphically illustrated than during the battle of Otumba. After they had succeeded in escaping a death trap in Tenochtitlan, Cortés led his troops north around Lake Xaltocan to Otumba located near the ancient ruins of Teotihuacan. Crossing a broad open plain, he was suddenly surrounded by an army of over 10,000 Aztecs. Exhausted and outnumbered, Cortés could do little but make a last stand. Soon he began to realize that the troops were being coordinated by a signal unit under the command of the Cihuacoatl or Snake Woman priest (7). Cortés boldly mounted his horse, charged through the oncoming Aztec army and cut down the Cihuacoatl. The effect was devastating. Not only were the Aztec troops demoralized by this desperate gamble, but they appear to have been unable to coordinate any more effective movement than to withdraw in total confusion. Later the Tlaxcaltecas presented the principal signal banner called the xopilli or "claw" device to Cortés in honor of his heroism.

In the years preceding the arrival of the Spaniards, omens in the form of bizarre celestial phenomena were witnessed and interpreted as signs of disaster. (Author's illustration from the *Florentine Codex*)

PLATE H: AN AZTEC SQUADRON SURPRISES THE HUAXTECS (AD 1454)

The Aztecs frequently employed a ruse, pretending to retreat in order to draw an enemy into an area especially prepared for ambush. When Motecuhzoma I faced a particularly fearsome army of Huaxtecs during his invasion of northern Veracruz, he ordered 2,000 troops to dig holes and conceal themselves under straw. The regular army then executed a successful feint at their center and began to disengage in retreat. The eager Huaxtecs followed in hot pursuit. Once they had passed into their midst, the secret army then literally rose from the ground and slaughtered the terrified enemy. Such war by deception was war by evasion; it was only executed successfully with careful planning, effective signaling, and perfect unit maneuvering. The Huaxtecs spoke a language closely related to that of the Maya of Central America but linguists still debate when they actually established themselves on Mexico's Gulf Coast. The Aztecs described them as frightening in their appearance with heads purposefully elongated or flattened having had their skulls bound as infants. Some had their teeth filed to points and many sported intricate tattoos. Many shunned the maxtlatl or breech clout, and they were accused of being lascivious drunkards. According to one legend Tezcatlipoca seduced the daughter of the King of Tollan by posing as a Huaxtec chili seller, the "chili" in mind referring to the Huaxtec's member.

PLATE I: TLAHUICOL DEFENDS HIMSELF IN GLADIATORIAL COMBAT BEFORE THE GREAT TEMPLE

Tlahuicol was a Tlaxcalan captain, sworn enemy of the Aztecs and their hated empire. He was captured and, due to his high rank, forced to participate in the ritual of gladiatorial combat before the Great Temple at Tenochtitlan. Armed only with mock weapons, his wits, and his fists, he succeeded in single-handedly killing no fewer than eight heavily armed jaguar and eagle warriors. He was subsequently offered a command position in the Imperial army. He declined declaring it to be an insult and voluntarily offered himself in sacrifice to the Aztec war-god Huitzilopochtli whose temple looms in the background. The unusual ritual garb with which Tlahuicol is dressed is the raiment of a war god known as Xipe Totec. Ritual combats were immensely popular. They brought the reality of combat home to a people who had invested so much in food and materiel, much less risked the very lives of their sons. Large circular stones thought to have been employed for gladiatorial combat are displayed in Mexico's National Museum of Anthropology and the Museum of the Great Temple. Both portray images of an Aztec emperor dressed as Huitzilopochtli capturing the gods of enemy city states. By sponsoring festival sculpture of this kind, the huey tlatoani clearly sought to combine spectacular showmanship with personal propaganda by reminding the audience of his role as the representative of Tenochtitlan's mightiest warrior. Military success packaged in this way appealed to patriotic and imperialist impulses in the public while providing a potent form of entertainment garnering popular admiration and gratitude.

According to legend, Quetzalcoatl (left) founded Tula and ruled as high priest there until he fell under the spell of his rivals Tezcatlipoca and Huitzilopochtli (right). Tricked into committing acts of drunkenness and incest, Quetzalcoatl was shamed before his people and driven out of the city. After founding a new cult center at Cholula, the man-god journeyed to the coast of Veracruz and embarked on a raft of serpents vowing to return one day and reclaim his kingdom from his rivals. Hero legends became the means by which Mesoamerican elites cross-cut differences in language and customs among their people and facilitated international alliance building. But like all great religious traditions, the teachings included apocalyptic prophecies that allowed the disenfranchised to express dissent as well. (Author's illustration from the *Florentine Codex*)

Cortés is presented with the ritual dress of the god Quetzalcoatl whose divine representative he was proclaimed to be. (Author's illustration from the *Florentine Codex*)

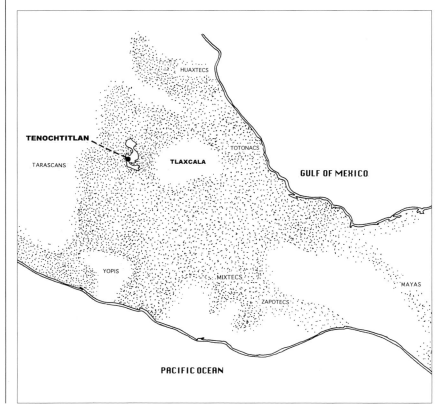

By 1519, the Aztecs had succeeded in dominating much of Central and Southern Mexico. Only Tlaxcala had remained unconquered. (Author's illustration)

PLATE J: THE SIEGE OF TENOCHTITLAN (AD 1521)

After two years of failed negotiations, war, and plague, the Aztecs had elected a new emperor, Cuauhtemoc, and began to fortify Tenochtitlan in preparation for a siege by 50,000 troops from Tlaxcala, Huexotzinco, Cholula, among other city states, together with their Spanish allies. The enemy attacked the city by both land and water. But once they had broken into the city, they quickly found themselves trapped within the labyrinth of city streets and canals. Many were lured into dead ends where they were easily crushed to death by stones and rubble cast down by troops positioned on the roofs of buildings. Those who sought to hide or pillage became lost in the mazes of small rooms and patios of private dwellings. Here an Aztec strike force has simultaneously broken through the timber roof and plaster walls of an apartment complex to mercilessly entrap and hack a Tlaxcalan and his Spanish ally to pieces. The Spaniard is a captain and master swordsman. The Tlaxcalan

wears the red and white head band of a nobleman and holds equal rank. His steel sword is a prized gift from the Spaniard. While bowmen pin the enemy down from above, two Aztec warriors have succeeded in breaking through the adobe brick walls of the room to surprise and corner the enemy. One is a noblemen identifiable by his ehuatl or tunic. The other is a warrior dressed in a tlahuiztli and helmet representing a legendary flaming coyote. Such strategic use of the urban setting forced Cortés to first retreat and then to initiate the siege all over again only by dismantling Tenochtitlan house by house in what would become the longest continuous battle in history.

The four tlatoque of Tlaxcala seek an alliance by offering their daughters in marriage together with gifts of dowry to the Spaniards. Cortés presides over the negotiations attended by his mistress, La Malinche. (Author's illustration from the *Lienzo de Tlaxcala*)

Quitlauhtique

INDEX

COMPANION SERIES FROM OSPREY

MEN-AT-ARMS

An unrivalled source of information on the organization, uniforms and equipment of the world's fighting men, past and present. The series covers hundreds of subjects spanning 5,000 years of history. Each 48-page book includes concise texts packed with specific information, some 40 photos, maps and diagrams, and eight color plates of uniformed figures.

ELITE

Detailed information on the uniforms and insignia of the world's most famous military forces. Each 64-page book contains some 50 photographs and diagrams, and 12 pages of full-color artwork.

NEW VANGUARD

Comprehensive histories of the design, development and operational use of the world's armored vehicles and artillery. Each 48-page book contains eight pages of full-color artwork including a detailed cutaway.

CAMPAIGN

Concise, authoritative accounts of history's decisive military encounters. Each 96-page book contains over 90 illustrations including maps, orders of battle, color plates, and three-dimensional battle maps.

ORDER OF BATTLE

The most detailed information ever published on the units which fought history's great battles. Each 96-page book contains comprehensive organization diagrams supported by ultra-detailed color maps. Each title also includes a large fold-out base map.

AIRCRAFT OF THE ACES

Focuses exclusively on the elite pilots of major air campaigns, and includes unique interviews with surviving aces sourced specifically for each volume. Each 96-page volume contains up to 40 specially commissioned artworks, unit listings, new scale plans and the best archival photography available.

COMBAT AIRCRAFT

Technical information from the world's leading aviation writers on the aircraft types flown. Each 96-page volume contains up to 40 specially commissioned artworks, unit listings, new scale plans and the best archival photography available.